Generis
PUBLISHING

Debating the contesting memories of slavery

Continental Africans and the Africans of the Diaspora

Dr. Ousseynou SY

Copyright © 2021 Dr. Ousseynou SY
Copyright © 2021 Generis Publishing

All rights reserved. This book or any portion thereof may not be reproduced or used in any manner whatsoever without the written permission of the publisher except for the use of brief quotations in a book review.

Title: Debating the contesting memories of slavery, Continental Africans and the Africans of the Diaspora

ISBN: 978-1-63902-432-2

Author: Dr. Ousseynou SY

Cover image: www.pixabay.com

Generis Publishing
Online orders: www.generis-publishing.com
Orders by email: info@generis-publishing.com

Dedication
In Memorium

I dedicate this modest work to my late parents. I also extend the dedication to my late spiritual father, Abdoul Aziz SY Dabakh.

Acknowledgements

First, I would like to thank Dr. Helena Woodard and Dr. Martin Kevorkian at the University of Texas at Austin. Both Profs Woodard and Kevorkian supervised my MA thesis and still continue to influence my research and academic career. This book is inspired by and draws greatly on Woodard's book *Slave Site on Display*. Reading *Slave Site on Display* drove me to rethink slavery from within, I mean interrogating the silenced African archives. Some of my arguments elaborate on some ideas raised in the book, such as the issues of authenticity and appropriation of the archives around slave sites, the enigma of forgiveness that slavery raises, and the complex co-existence between various historical narratives of slavery that researchers in diaspora and Africana studies have to sift through to understand slavery as a history and as a discourse.

I thank my staunch friend Dr. Mamadou Moustapha LY at Denver University, Colorado, US for sharing tirelessly documentations with me. Much the same is true with Eileen McGinnis at Saint Edward University, Austin, Texas. I also thank my nephew and colleague Ahmed Ndiaye for reading and making insightful comments that directed me toward more original lines of inquiry.

And finally, I would like to thank my family members: my dearest sister, Lika SY, and her late husband, El Hadji Yare Fall, my mother-in-law Ngoné Kébé. Other relatives and friends have greatly contributed in the creation of this project through their supports. Among those, I wish to thank Thierna Moctar Dia, and late Imam Mbaye Dia, my beloved adoptive father.

I dare not finish without thanking my late professors Dr. Mamadou Gaye and Dr. Mamadou Camara, two eminent scholars who supervised all my work in Senegal. I extend the gratitude to their longtime friend and colleague Prof. El Hadji Haby Sow, the first teacher who made me love words.

The last word of gratitude goes to my lovely wife for her support and patience, hoping that our son will do better than us.

Table of Contents

Acknowledgements 6
Epigraphs 8
Introduction 9
The Continental Africans and the Africans of the diaspora's memory of slavery 13
CODA 29
The repressed memory of slavery by some Africans of the diaspora 32
Slavery's answerability represented in African American literature 44
Conclusion 55
Sources cited 57

Epigraphs

Perhaps art will be the medium by which we can make our loss palpable to each other; perhaps it will be the medium of our eventual healing. (Sandra L. Richards, "Notes from the Road: Cultural Tourism to Slave Sites," 1999, p. 12)

L'HISTOIRE EST UN ROMAN DONT LE PEUPLE EST L'AUTEUR. (Afred de Vigny, *Les Grands Romans Historiques* Volume 15, Éditions de Crémille, Genéve, 1969, p.10)

HISTORY IS A NOVEL WHOSE AUTHOR IS THE PEOPLE. (My translation)

"Rather than invent a world, I want a different means to understand this one." Jena, Osman, *The Network* (Jena, Osman, *The Network*. Albany: Fence Books, 2011, p. 38)

Introduction

The desire to know and the unmeasurable pain of not being able to know.

When discussing slavery in her book *Slave Sites on Display*, Helena Woodard asks the following question: "...who bears the lion's share of responsibility of that trade." (p. 21) Through her inquiry, Woodard raises the question about the culpability for the Atlantic slave trade. Next to Woodard's question about shared responsibility about slavery, we can juxtapose Achille Mbembe's argument, in "African Modes of Self Writing," that Africans and African Americans don't share the same memory of slavery. He argues that there is on the side of the continental Africans "a significant ablation" (p. 20). Achille Mbembe poses his argument in these terms:

First, between the African-Americans' memory of slavery and that of continental Africans, there is a shadowy zone that conceals a deep silence: the silence of guilt and the refusal of Africans to face up to the troubling aspect of the crime that directly engages their own responsibility. For the fate of black slaves in modernity is not the solely result of the tyrannical will and cruelty of the Other--even though the latter is well-established. The other primitive signifier is the murder of brother by brother, 'the elision of the first syllable of the family name' (Lacan), in short, the divided city. (p. 20)

On this "shadowy zone that conceals a deep silence" is what this book endeavors to shed light. My claim here is that the silences of history have to be unmuted for the sake of 'devoir de mémoire' and also for the need of engaging a sincere international dialogue on shared responsibility in healing the wounds of slavery. I also contend that the only history that can be viewed as tragic or shameful is the one muted since it is most likely to repeat itself in one way or another.

Our modern human rights, political and theological sensibilities are to be horrified to see these 'wounded histories' (to use Nancy Peterson's term) such as genocide, ethnic cleansing, slavery, world war etc. repeat themselves. Indeed, as Derrida argues, in "On Cosmopolitanism and Forgiveness," if we were to blame each other for all the crimes against humanity that the world has seen no nation or people would be innocent enough to be either judge or mediator since "We are all heir, at least, to persons or events marked, in an essential, interior, ineffaceable fashion, by crimes against humanity." (p. 29). To create this space wherein dialogues about answerability and healing can occur, we need to know the historical truth. Revealing the historical truth is not only cathartic but also it can unblock the confusion between diaspora slave descendants and the continental Africans about what really happened and how it happened. Not being able to know engenders in itself a pain. That's why Woodard, quoting Vamik Volkan, talks about the infusion between the transgenerational transmission of injured selves with the memory of the ancestors' trauma. The unquenchable desire for historical truth of both diaspora slave descendants and regional Africans and the inability of the archives to render such a truth shows that the effects of slavery still linger. That's why Woodard writes, "I believe that the legacy that slavery leaves us is the way in which we view things beneath the surface, around the edges, and in the interstices" (p. 9) Because of this past that is never dead, that has not even been past, to paraphrase Faulker in *Requiem for a Nun*, reconstituting the historical truth is both cathartic and illuminating for the future. Reconstituting the historical truth boils down to erecting, metaphorically, a sort of *Sankofa* transatlantic slavery monument.

The *Sankofa* in Akan, Ghanaian culture, is a symbol of birth, renewal, and growth. The *Sankofa* can use the chaotic past as a stepping stone to a brighter future. Sankofa, as Christel N. Temple reminds us, literally means in Akan *"it is not taboo to fetch what is at risk of being left behind."* So, the Akans believe that there must be movement and new learning as time passes by. The erection of the *Sankofa* transatlantic slavery monument can create a potential space where forgiveness can be called for, reparations or political reorientations, and reconciliations be made. Yet to reconstitute the historical truth about slavery is not an easy endeavor since it requires a critical engagement with the "archive fever" (to use Derrida's term) or "the colossal failures in the archival records" (p. 4) as Woodard points out. By the "archive fever," Derrida means that the archives are inherently selective. The archive and the archivist are consumed by amnesia and obliviousness. As Richard Crownshaw writes, echoing Derrida, "'There is no preservation without destruction, "that which permits and conditions archivization.'" (p. 219) By "the colossal failures in the archival records", Woodard implies not only the selectivity of the archives, but also the authenticity of historical records and historical edifices like slave sites and other museums. To answer these questions about the reconstitution of the historical truth and the creation of a healing space of the different parties involved in the transnational crime under study here, what Hartman calls "the ethics of historical representation" (p.19) (as quoted by Markus Nehl in *Transnational Black Dialogue*) has to override the biased and self-exculpatory discourse.

I draw on both fiction and non-fiction scholarships on slavery, memory, history, culture and trauma to analyze the contesting memories of slavery between the Continental Africans and the Africans of the Diaspora and the dilemmas of creating a common healing space so as to exorcise the demons of the past. I will focus on Ralph Ellison's *Invisible Man* and *Juneteenth* and Toni Morrison's *Beloved* and *Paradise* to discuss the ideology of both blackwash and whitewash. By the ideology of blackwash, I mean the Africans' willed intention to silence their involvement or 'bystanderness' in the transatlantic slave trade. By the neologism 'bystanderness,' I mean the narratives of powerlessness vis-à-vis the Other that Africans often resort to disclaim their involvement.

The ideology of whitewash refers to the Americans' politics and processes of erasure of slavery. These four works of fiction, written in the tradition of recovering what Fredric Jameson calls "history as wound," will allow me to demonstrate that both Morrison and Ellison's texts bear historical tropes that participate in Hartman's "the ethics of historical representation." I mean both Ellison and Morrison's fiction engage directly with the issues of repressed and conflicting memories about slavery and the dilemmas of remembering and forgetting. Achille Mbembe's "African Modes of Self Writing" and Helena Woodard's *Slave Sites on Display* are the two major non-fiction scholarships that serve as a theoretical background. Mbembe's essay revolves mainly around the ideology of blackwash and its consequences in creating a genuine space for dialogue and healing. Woodard's book *Slave Sites on Display* examines the issues of authenticity in slave sites which I analyze as historical edifices that can greatly participate in reconstituting the historical truth. Woodard's book discusses also, through a contemporary "flash" moment approach, the issues of forgiveness and the legacy of slavery in the contemporary world. Indeed, slave forts are both historical artefacts and geopolitical spaces. Woodard sums up the twofold dimension of slave sites in these terms:

My contention is that conflicts between purveyors of a traditional archival, historical past and propagators of a symbolic memory for the present appropriately begin with slave forts in Africa and morph outwardly to slave sites elsewhere in the global community. In this capacity, they express the tenets of a virulent, cyclical slavery and offer new ways to rethink its meaning in the modern world. (p. 21)

As a theoretical framework then, Woodard's book can rightly shed light not only on the issues of authenticity around the slave forts and the conflation between history and memory, but also the manipulation and appropriation of the archives. As she asks when scrutinizing Gorée, Senegal's slave fort, quoting Carolyn J. Mooney, "...Who governed the memory about what happened at that fort, and who is officially charged with archiving that memory." (p. 31). Sandra Richards sums up the interplay of various historical narratives operating at slave sites in these terms:

Third, slave sites are potentially contested spaces where a variety of historical narratives and ideological agendas are enacted. For some, slavery is one, albeit painful chapter in a much longer, more glorious human history; for others the memory of slavery is not quite history but rather, a catalyst to unleashing concerns about contemporary powerlessness; and for still others, though slavery - and specifically African complicity in the trade - cannot be denied, more important is the forging of economic bonds between African-descended peoples in the United States and Africans on the continent. (p. 11)

On this enactment of various historical narratives and ideological agendas is what this present research intends to lay emphasis as well. It argues that the various historical narratives and ideological agendas result from a difference in the sentimental attachments to historical injury of slavery. Therefore, the African unifying narratives of common ancestry fall short in fixing the historical injury. The latter calls for an appeal for recognition which the narratives of descent and the various ideological agendas can't undermine.

The Continental Africans and the Africans of the diaspora's memory of slavery:

> We cannot escape our past, for it continues to influence our present mental processes. Memories we would put away as too painful to face haunt us ceaselessly in our unconscious minds. We try to forget the past; we may cover it over with more benign and tolerable screen memories. But the unrequited prompting of the past cripples our reckoning with the present. (539)

Patrick Hutton explains in this opening passage from his essay "The History Teacher" that the past acts on the present. As a victim of trauma, our past memories can't be put aside, and if we succeed in doing so we will suffer critically searching for our true being and identity. Therefore, if a community went through the same trauma, there can't be a *décalage* in their experience of the event. And if there is a *décalage* then their sentimental attachments to the event diverge. I deliberately use the French word *décalage* because of its plurality of meanings and subtle nuances within these meanings. Markus Nehl in *Transnational Black Dialogues*, quoting Edwards, defines *décalage* as "the kernel of precisely that which cannot be transferred or exchanged, the received biases that refuse to pass over when one crosses the water." (p. 49) He further explains that "*décalage* refers to an incongruity, a fissure in time or a gap in space." (p. 49) To the meanings, we can irrefutably add: delay and distance. In the light of this theoretical framework, if there is a *décalage* in a community's experience of the same trauma, then there is a gap, fissure, or distance in their sentimental attachments to historical injury. The transatlantic slave trade epitomizes such an event. The continental Africans and the Africans of the diaspora don't share the same sentimental attachments to historical injury of slavery. This fact is brought to the fore when Woodard contrasts the regional Africans' attachment to slave forts with that of the Africans of the diaspora. She writes:

> Many visiting diaspora slave descendants overlook the impoverished condition of local inhabitants and focus instead on the fort's connection with slavery, while those in surrounding communities,

struggling to improve their lives, ignore both the slave forts and the slave descendants that gather there. (p. 29)

Woodard underscores here that the sanctity and attention that the diaspora slave descendants have toward to slave forts differ from that of regional Africans. In Woodard's quotation, the attention of the regional Africans to the slave forts is deflected by poverty. Yet behind this poverty that seemingly hides the regional African's lack of devotion to the slave forts lies a deep *décalage* in historical injury. This *décalage* in historical injury, due to a break in continuity between slavery as experienced, lived, learned, and taught in both sides of the Atlantic, cannot be equated with amnesia, but with a repressed memory. Indeed, mourning is a healing process that never ends, only its intensity decreases. In this respect, Patrick Hutton reminds us in his essay "Recent Scholarship on Memory and History", "Remembering is a strategy of mourning, of letting go of a particular past, but slowly, critically, respectfully of how it served us, for good or ill." (p. 543) In the light of Hutton's assertion, we can argue that the Africans of the diaspora and the regional Africans have a different historical memory of slavery. The former, as unencumbered heirs, still hold a firm retention of the past while the latter, occupying a limbo status, let a *décalage* set in between them and that past. The sentimental attachments to historical injury of slavery being different, the continental Africans and the Africans of the diaspora can't have the same memory of slavery since, as Mbembe argues, "the temporalities of servitude and misery" (p. 20) differ greatly.

Therefore, this ruptured continuity accounts, in part, for the difference in the sentimental attachments to historical injury of slavery. To have the same consciousness and memory of slavery, the continental Africans and the Africans of the diaspora have to endure the same suffering or severing, trauma, absence and loss. And Woodard's portrayal of the regional Africans' attachment to the slave forts in contrast to that of Africans of the diaspora underscores such a *décalage* in memory and consciousness of slavery. There is an untranslatability of memory since the Africans of the diaspora still endure the sequels of slavery in their transplanted soil while for the continental Africans slavery is more or less part of a distant past that they still have to reconcile themselves with. Consequently, the memory of slavery of the Africans of the diaspora and that of the regional Africans move poles asunder. The poverty can Woodard identifies as the plague that makes the slave fort inhabitants ignore them and the forts is rather a symptom of blackwash than amnesia. There is a dissonance between the two; a dissonance that recalls the African father and his three children in Caryl Phillips's *Crossing the River*. I turn here to fiction to put a finger on the silences of history since creative art is an efficient device to articulate the inarticulable as our first opening epigraph suggests. When analyzing the relationship between the African father and his three children, in "Haunting the African Diaspora", Maria Rice Bellamy writes "While the father's words attempt to provide an explanation for his actions and give meaning of the suffering of his children, the reader is left with the realization that he speaks into the void, to children who cannot hear him." (p. 129) Similarly, these dispersed three children can't have the same memory of the event as their father once they reach the far bank of the river. Also, as time passes by there will be a memory *décalage* between the African father and his dispersed children. Caryl Phillips's *Crossing the River* can help better explain the encounter between the diaspora slave descendants and the regional Africans that Woodard describes at the slave forts.

Also, another narrative of blackwash around slave forts that engenders a memory *décalage* is the inability to get access to the historicity of slave forts. There is a narrative of blackwash that obscures the debates, academic or public, about the authenticity of slave sites. About Senegal's slave fort, various contesting ideologies defend or reject the fort as a site for slave trade and deportation. Was the slave fort built to house the concubines of European slave traders? Was it a major or minor holding cell for enslaved Africans? Or is the slave fort just a myth? Answering these questions which raise irrefutably other strings of questions requires a researcher's life span. On top of these questions, there is a wave of business tourism around slave sites that enacts its own political and ideological agenda. How to get access to the historical truth in the midst of these opaque archival narratives? In the midst of this archival opacity, slavery becomes open to appropriation and manipulation by its various stakeholders. In this respect, Woodard writes:

> The griot at the House of Slaves and site organizers for Equiano at Birmingham, for example, represent a group collective empowered to transform slavery by privileging certain symbolic memory practices over archival historical records, thus (re)shaping the politics of race as ideology. Through public relations and marketing strategies, as well as perspectives formed from a remembered or restructured past, these sites organizers and spectators refigure slavery" (p. 44)

Because of these various political and ideological agendas, slavery becomes an heteroglot opinion that recalls what Bakhtin labels "heteroglossia," defined as conflict of voices in a text:

> As a living, socio-ideological concrete thing, as heteroglot opinion, language, for the individual consciousness, lies on the borderline between oneself and the other. The word in language is half someone else's. It becomes "one's own" only when the speaker populates it with his own intention, his own accent, when he appropriates the word, adapting it to his own semantic and expressive intention (293).

In the light of Bakhtin's theory of "heteroglossia," slavery becomes a heteroglot ideology that people can appropriate, regardless of the archival truth, to feed their political and ideological narratives. I mean these various narratives about slavery shows that memory is being historicized to the point that it has jammed the archival narratives, and thereby superseding history. The memory *décalage* of slavery between regional Africans and Africans of the diaspora results particularly from this enactment of slavery that renders memory historic.

Moreover, by historicizing memory to the detriment of archival narrative, all chances of reconstituting the historical truth narrows down to impossibility. The historicized memory of slavery transmits a historical narrative of slavery that is not utterly inaccurate but incomplete in many regards. The historicized memory of slavery enacts the historical truth. In this respect, Woodard talks about the performance of Joseph N'diaye (Gorée's legendary curator) at the slave site of Gorée in this passage:

The fort's role in the Atlantic slave trade, in tandem with the sojourner's mission, is inextricable from N'diaye's performance, because he has inured himself in the historicity of the slave past. Without his very presence and the narrative that he dispenses - or that of his successor - the site stands as a fixed symbol, an immovable object. (p. 33)

The narratives about slavery that N'diaye dispenses lie between historicized memory and archival narrative. The visitor of the site is not provided with archival documents to engage critically with N'diaye's historicized memory narrative. Much the same is true with the curator or tour guide at the African Burial Ground in New York: Douglass Massenburg. Woodard relates Massenburg's performance in these terms: "Through performance and articulation in a "flash" moment-in-time, Massenburg transformed from tour guide into messianic sermonizer, theatrical performer, and oral historian perhaps reminiscent of Joseph N'diaye at Gorée Island's House of Slaves in Senegal." (p. 47) Much like in Gorée's slave site, history tends to be oralized in the African Burial Ground in New York by Massenburg. In so doing, the historical truth becomes a theatre. This theatricality of the historical truth leads further to a confusion and disjunction among the different actors involved in the crime under study, which recalls the scene in Rousseau's accusing of Marion of theft in *Les Confessions*. In the light of Rousseau's text, the failure to confess or the refusal to confess or the false accusations jam the historicity of slavery, and thereby damages its cultural inheritance.

Another question about Joseph N'diaye's slavery narrative that Woodard does not elaborate on is where does the narrative of slavery that Joseph N'diaye relate come from? Is he drawing, for example, on colonial library (bibliothèque coloniale)? Colonial library, as Étienne Smith and Céline Labrune articulate, refers to the body of information and knowledge produced by Africans themselves but that colonial authorities had to validate before archivization. This point is worth bringing up since the colonial library by its very nature suffers from censorship and therefore, it has to be made whole and contrasted with the historical truth from the various historical discourses built around memory or driven by particular political agendas. The archived colonial library typifies the 'archive fever' or 'the colossal failures in the archival record'. Censorship, recuperative, and other political agendas are enacted in the colonial library. Because of this, Joseph N'diaye's slavery narrative has to go at some point against the grain of the colonial library in order to be complete. But was he or is his successor entitled to do so? Both Derrida and Woodard pit the archives as a pre-occupied and contested space that they approach with interrogative and interrogating voices. When their skepticism of the archives is applied to the colonial library, it becomes clear that the historical truth lies, in part, in the unvalidated knowledge or information. But, where are they? Inside every colonial library in West Africa, there are labyrinths of archives suppressed. In the midst of these politics and processes of blackwashing and whitewashing, the first thing to be damaged is the ethics governing archives.

Another author who foregrounds how slavery has been turned into a heteroglot ideology is Laura T. Murphy in *Metaphor and the Slave Trade in West African Literature*. Murphy illustrates how the slave forts in Ghana are blackwashed by the government. The slave forts are used to house other administrative offices. This indicates both a politics and process of erasure and a willed intent to put aside what no longer matters (the same strategy is deployed in *Invisible Man* by the white trustees, I will pick up this point later) and participates in reinforcing a memory *décalage* of slavery between regional Africans and Africans of the diaspora. Murphy describes this blackwash of the Ghanaian slave forts in this passage:

> The people who live in the cities and villages surrounding the old posts harbor a wide range of ideas about what the structures symbolize. Perhaps the most significant of the structures is Christiansborg Castle (also known as Osu), which peeks out over the edge of the Atlantic on the coast of Accra. Originally built by the Danish in 1661, it was transferred to the British and later used as the home of their colonial government. When Ghana gained its independence in 1957, Christiansborg became the seat of the new postcolonial government, and in 1960 its newly elected president, Kwame Nkrumah, took up residence there. It remained the seat of government until 2008, when President John Kufuor, responding to controversy over the tainted historical implications of governing from a slave castle, moved into a newly constructed, federally funded $50 million presidential palace called Golden Jubilee House. President John Atta Mills returned to Osu Castle after his election in 2009, ignoring historical arguments and favoring austerity instead, citing the enormous expense of maintaining the residence at Golden Jubilee (now officially renamed Flagstaff House). Today, after that short and highly politicized hiatus, Ghana's presidential residence is located at Osu Castle once again, and access to the castle is strictly monitored. (pp. 11-12)

Murphy further comments on the palimpsestic legacy of the slave fort in Ghana in these terms:

> The castle continues, through successive governments, to signify the inheritance of political power - whether that power is exploitative or benevolent, foreign or indigenous. The legacy of exploitation that marks the site is central to continuing public debates over the propriety of fixing the seat of government at a site haunted by the most devastating reminders of violence in the nation's history, but the signification of power is so convincing that president after president returns to it as their own seat of political authority. Proponents of

> transforming the castle into a museum seek a corresponding transformation of the concept of political power in the country, which they think could be effected by relegating the slave trade and its monuments to a narrative of Ghana's past, exiling the trade from the landscape of contemporary politics. (p. 12)

As Murphy highlights, the ruling Ghanaian elites, who to many extents fully embody the former colonizers (I will open a CODA to elaborate on this), are interested in suppressing the historicity of the slave fort. While those who advocate the preservation of the historic site are in the minority and they lack agency. The will of the ruling Ghanaian elites to wipe out the slave sites emphasizes the difference in the sentimental attachments to historical injury of slavery between regional Africans and Africans of the diaspora. The Africans of the diaspora invest their money, time, and risk their lives to visit these slave forts that the Ghanaians want to blackwash. The Africans of the diaspora's memory and consciousness of slavery and that of regional Africans fall into "...the tension between continuity and discontinuity, similarity and difference that characterizes diasporic life" (p. 44) as Markus Nehl writes in *Transnational Black Dialogues*. But this "tension between continuity and discontinuity, similarity and difference" characterizes also an inner difference between regional Africans in regard to slavery. Some regional Africans have more interest in removing the slave forts than others. Also, this difference in memory and consciousness of slavery shows that within the regional African themselves there is a contesting memory of slavery. This is due to the fact that the ancestors of some Africans are more answerable than others. Murphy puts a finger on this African answerability when she writes:

> Even if we step away from the obvious and institutionalized "sites of memory" such as the slave castles, West African people have developed their own ways of explaining and describing the history of the transatlantic slave trade to themselves and their descendants understand the devastating impact of the slave trade as well as African involvement and complicity in it. (p. 19)

In light of Murphy's clarification, it becomes clear that there is a tension between Africans about how to reconcile themselves with that side of the slave trade history that points a finger at them. Woodard elaborates on this issue when analyzing President Obama's visit to the slave fort in Ghana. She writes:

> For diaspora slave descendants, Obama's visit represented a symbolic return that perhaps mirrored for them the possibility of overcoming the past. But, as I have previously stated, the president's historic visit to Cape Coast also exposes a "mythology of return" that implicates those slave descendants as well as African inhabitants who project vastly different experiences and hence different relationships with the slave past. (p. 29)

Both Murphy and Woodard underscore the contesting memory of slavery within the continent. This explains probably why the Ghanaian ruling elites and the population fight over the control of memory of slave forts. This internal contesting memory between Africans shows that some Africans like the Africans of the diaspora still carry a postmemory of slavery. But obviously not to the same degree like the Africans of the diaspora. As we recall, postmemory is a living cross-generational remembering process. Postmemory implies that there is no rupture between the trauma of the ancestors and their descendants who inherit that trauma. Marianne Hirsch who theorizes postmemory uses photographs to analyze how the memories of the victims of trauma can be passed on to the next generations to the point that it becomes memories of their own. To Hirsch, postmemory describes:

> The relationship of children of survivors of cultural or collective trauma to the experiences that they 'remember' only as the narratives and images with which they grow up, but that are so powerful, so monumental, as to constitute memories of their own right. (p.9)

Much like photographs that salvage and preserve memories, slave sites have the same functionality. The slave site functions both as a bequest and a substitute memory or compensatory memory that is meant to offset a historical amnesia or erasure. The slave site enables some sort of historical continuum for the Africans of the diaspora. Woodard describes it as both womb and tomb; and Murphy elaborates on this metaphor in these terms, "The castle itself plays a dual symbolic role of this elegy: It signifies the site from which Africans were expelled from their homes as well as the site at which, generations later, their descendants (both literal and symbolic) will finally find their ancestral home" (p. 14)

The other rationale that justifies the difference in the sentimental attachments to historical injury of slavery between the diaspora slave descendants and the continental Africans is that in this transnational crime, the Africans are seen as either bystanders or allegedly accomplices or even perpetrators. Therefore, the memory of trauma, absence, and loss can't be similar. In other words, the diaspora slave descendants are the sole victims in this crime while the continental Africans occupy an ambiguous posture. To emphasize this complex standing of the continental Africans, Mbembe writes:

> As a result, the appeal to race as the moral and political basis of solidarity will always depend, to some extent, on a mirage of consciousness so long as continental Africans have not rethought the slave trade and the other forms of slavery, not merely as a catastrophe that befell them, but also as the product of a history they have played an active part in shaping through the way in which they have treated each other. (p. 20)

Indeed, if we analyze slavery through the lens of the human rights theory that argues that each crime against humanity can be apprehended using the three actors of victims, perpetrators, and bystanders, continental Africans fall into a limbo state. Derrida uses this human rights theory to discuss the South African Truth and Reconciliation Commission. Drawing on this human rights theory to analyze shared responsibility of slavery leaves the continental Africans in limbo, unable to incriminate the Other without pointing a finger at themselves. That's why in his 2009 interview with Anderson Cooper during his visit to the slave fort in Ghana, President Obama describes slavery as one of those crimes that should never be approached as a situation in which "there's simply a victim and a victimizer and that's the end of the story." As long as slavery is approached through this sole victim and victimizer paradigm, the "shadowy zone that conceals a deep silence" that Mbembe warns us about will remain. In other words, as long as this "shadowy zone that conceals a deep silence" persists the continental Africans' memory of slavery will collide with that of diaspora slave descendants. Also, the contesting memory of Africans themselves will also persist as long as this "shadowy zone that conceals a deep silence" is not cleared. The reconstitution of the historical truth will enable the regional Africans to pull themselves out of this dual limbo state.

Mbembe in the preceding quotation urges us to go back in time of history. In the XV and XVIII centuries, Africa was made of kingdoms. We had major powerful kingdoms like the kingdoms of Benin, Nri, the Ghana Empire, the Mali Empire, the Shonghay Empire ect. These kingdoms used to wage wars between them. The war soldiers in these inter-kingdom fights were often either kept as slaves or sold as slaves to the Europeans. This is what Mbembe alludes to when he talks about "the other forms of slavery." This internal slavery precedes the Atlantic slave trade and is often overlooked by the African historians. Much the same is true with the internal slavery practiced by the Arabs, the Berbers, that precedes the Atlantic slave trade as well. Henry Louis Gates, in his article "Ending the Slavery Blame-Game" points out that on the scale that slavery occurred, it has to have involved Africans. In this respect, he writes:

> While we are familiar with the role played by the United States and the European colonial powers like Britain, France, Holland, Portugal and Spain, there is very little discussion of the role Africans themselves played. And that role, it turns out, was a considerable one, especially for the slave-trading kingdoms of western and central Africa. These included the Akan of the kingdom of Asante in what is now Ghana, the Fon of Dahomey (now Benin), the Mbundu of Ndongo in modern Angola and the Kongo of today's Congo, among several others.

It is clearly from this particular historical context of early African kingdoms that slavery originates. It is consequently in such a divided city that the "murder of brother by brother", as Mbembe argues, can take place. Because of all these historical reasons that Mbembe and Gates lay bare, the regional Africans and Africans of the diaspora can't have the same sentimental attachments to the historical injury of slavery. Therefore, their memories of slavery can't dovetail and overlap. A fictional example that could illustrate this difference of sentimental attachments to historical injury of slavery between the continental Africans and the Africans of the diaspora is Baby Suggs' remembrance of her eight absented children. As we recall Baby Suggs is the matriarch of the community in *Beloved*:

> Great God, she thought, where do I start? Get someone to write old Whitlow. See who took Patty and Rosa Lee. Someone name Dunn got Ardelia and went West, she heard. No point in trying for Tyree or John. They cut thirty years ago and, if she searched too hard and they were hiding, finding them would do them more harm than good.

> Nancy and Famous died in a ship off the Virginia Coast before it set sail for Savannah. That much she knew. The overseer at Whitlow's place brought her the news, more from a wish to have his way with her than from the kindness of his heart. (p.169)

The experience of loss and absence that Baby Suggs feels about her runaway and scattered children can be likened to the memory of slavery that Africans of the diaspora have. Nothing can fill up the absence of Baby Suggs' runaway and scattered children. As Connor points out quoting Derrida, "'quelque-chose manque à sa place, mais le manque n'y manque jamais' – 'some-thing is missing from its place, but the lack is never missing from it.'" (p. 2) The lack that is never missing from its place is like the sentimental attachments to historical injury of slavery. It is there and it varies across the Atlantic. As it stands out in the quotation, Baby Suggs' desire to remember and her unbearable pain of remembering her dismembered family clash each other. Absence triggers here a memory that is quiescent and yet active. Such a type of memory describes most memories of slavery of the Africans of the diaspora. In other words, there is a permanent loss or absence that engenders memorabilia; a wound that refuses to heal.

Yet if Baby Suggs were involved in dismembering her own children, it becomes obvious that her sentimental attachments to this historical event would change. Instead of being keen on remembering, she would be prone to forget. In other words, instead of a lack that is never missing from its place, that lack will be filled up by amnesia, annihilation, or denial or remorse. Such an amnesia or denial characterizes the memory of slavery of continental Africans. This amnesic memory that tries to erase the past recalls what Jennifer Eichstedt and Stephen Small call, in *Representations of Slavery, Race and Ideology in the Southern Plantation Museums*, 'symbolic annihilation' which is a discursive practice that consists in representing the enslaved and their experience in "a perfunctory and fleeting way." (p. 107) This 'symbolic annihilation' works towards the erasure or marginalization of the institution or experience of slavery. The Ghanaian ruling elites who have decided to renovate and turn the slave castle into a presidential castle have wittingly or unwittingly recourse to this 'symbolic annihilation'. We can open here a parenthesis to talk about this 'symbolic annihilation' of the institution or experience of slavery in America drawing on Ellison's *Invisible Man*.

Ralph Ellison's *Invisible Man* deconstructs the 'symbolic annihilation' that has rendered the African American history invisible from the national archives.

Ellison purposefully sets the Negro college in an old plantation. Thereby he begins a palimpsestic narrative that represents the college both as an "Eden" (because it favors the education of blacks and their social uplift) and its location in an old plantation offers an ironic and paradoxical lens through which we can read two layers of historical narrative that move poles asunder. As the narrator drives the wealthy white trustee of the college, Mr. Norton, around the campus, the reader is exposed to this superimposition or juxtaposition of historical narratives: the narrator contrasts the edenic description of the college opening chapter two with this passage that describes the other sides of the campus:

> We were passing a collection of shacks and log cabins now, bleached white and warped by the weather. Sun-tortured shingles lay on the roofs like decks of water-soaked cards spread out to dry. The houses consisted of two squares rooms joined together by a common floor and roof with a porch in between........
> It was an old cabin with its chinks filled with chalk-white clay, with bright new shingles patching its roofs (46).

Through this palimpsestic narrative, Ellison crafts a historical narrative that binds past and present into a revisionist fabric of history. He underscores the importance of the past throughout the text.

Significantly enough, by setting the college in an old plantation, Ellison recovers the wounded history of his community that the college trustees try to wipe out through the ideology of whitewash. As the above quotation informs us there was "a collection of shacks and log cabins now, bleached white and warped by the weather" (46). This palimpsestic narration not only presents two conflicting superimposed versions of history, but also moves back and forth through time. This particular narration, which can also be read as a mise-en-abime narrative since it inscribes stories within stories, histories within histories, and unfolds the historical conditions that have rendered minority histories invisible from the mainstream American culture. Ellison presents a countermemory or counterhistory discourse that is against the erasure of the wounds of the past. The sequels of the past that Ellison brings to the fore in his narrative constitute a symbolic texture that is against the annihilation of the past. Therefore Ellison, as a *Sankofa* advocate, invites the official ideologies of the America nation-state to apprehend history with a *Sankofa* mindset.

The same politics and process of whitewashing that the college white trustees deploy in Ellison's text operates within the continental African's memory of slavery. As we have already showed, the Ghanaian elites' endeavor to turn the former slave castle into a presidential castle mimics the 'symbolic annihilation' in Ellison's text. There is a 'symbolic annihilation' of slavery that manifests itself in the African public and academic discourse. The 'symbolic annihilation' of slavery in the African public and academic discourse reveals also the dis-ease and discomfort for people to cope with wounded histories. Nancy Peterson sums up this kind of epilepsy (loss of consciousness) in these terms: "some things are unspoken because reigning ideologies do not consider them worthy of notice. Other things are unspeakable because they are too traumatic to be remembered" (52). As Nancy Peterson argues here, remembering can be so traumatic that people prefer to forget or 'the reigning ideologies' (the historiographers, the archivists, and the policy makers) prefer to simply suppress this traumatic side of history. This 'symbolic annihilation' of the African reigning ideologies of slavery creates an imbalance in the African representation of slavery in literature, national dialogue, and school curricula. Drawing on Achille Mbembe and Ghanaian poet Kwadwo Opoku-Agyemang, Woodard points out that whenever slavery is referenced in school curricula, "discussions about slavery heavily favor the point of view that befits colonial domination" (p. 28) This politics and process of annihilation creates a *décalage* in the sentimental attachments to historical injury of slavery between the continental Africans and the Africans of the diaspora. The politics and process of annihilation brings forth a closure that prevents the engagement of a frank dialogue about slavery and consequently undermines the racial affinities. An instance in Ellison's text that could illustrate this point is the doctors who refuse to see the wound in Brother Tarp's limp.

Brother Tarp is an embodiment and living memory of his community's wounded history. He has an indelible stigma that records the unvoiced traumatic history of slavery. Yet, the doctors can't see this stigma. Brother Tarp delves into his painful past to excavate his buried memories about his enslaved life that the doctors want to suppress. Here runs the passage as he narrates it to Invisible Man:

> You see, I was down there for a long time before I come up here, and when I did come up they were after me. What I mean is, I had to escape, I had to come a-running."

> "[……..] You noticed this limp I got?"
> *Well, I wasn't always lame, and I'm not really now 'cause the doctors can't find anything wrong with this leg. They say it's sound as a piece of steel.* What I mean is I got this limp from dragging a chain … and after nineteen years I haven't been able to stop dragging my leg (387). (emphasis added)

It's obvious in Ellison's text that the doctors who refuse to see the wound in Brother Tarp's limp won't make any diagnosis and ultimately prescribe a proper remedy. But by narrating his story of limp, Brother Tarp constructs a powerful historical narrative capable of filling in the holes in the mainstream American history. Through this passage, there is an acknowledgement that a wounded and traumatic history leaves always the victimizer in discomfort or epilepsy. Because of this discomfort and unspeakability that results from the wounds of the past, a policy of 'symbolic annihilation' is sometimes deployed on both sides of the Atlantic.

Laura Murphy discusses, too, this 'symbolic annihilation' of slavery in Africa literature. Woodard dexterously sums up Murphy's argument in these terms:

> Laura Murphy argues persuasively in *Metaphor and the Slave Trade in West African Literature* that rather than ignore slavery in their literature, many African writers represent it "differently" through metaphors that do not follow protracted neo-slave narrative form, especially as popularized in the Americas. She finds that slavery indeed remains embedded in family oral traditions in local African communities, landscape, and stories. Murphy insists that slave remembrance in African literature and memory studies varies and does not necessarily project the slavery-to-emancipation themes that are prevalent in African American and other Western publications. And yet there is supreme irony in discussions about the absence of overt references to or discussions of slavery in African literature while an explosive "heritage tourism" industry in public culture highlights the very forts and slave castles where slaves were imprisoned prior to transportation across the Atlantic in the Middle Passage. (p. 28)

Both Woodard and Murphy draw our attention to two critical points in the continental African's memory of slavery. The continental African's memory of slavery is repressed when it comes to discussing the history of slavery as it really happened, which would probably engage to some extent their answerability or 'bystanderness'. Not to openly debate slavery even in school curricula and African literature shows a tactful strategy for the African education policy makers to shirk this thorny issue. Murphy analyzes how slavery is metaphorized in the literary production of West African writers instead of being dealt with in substance. For example, in Morrison's *Beloved*, slavery is given substance through the ghost child that returns to haunt her community. Such a representation of slavery does not exist in West African literature. Why not a reversed Beloved who comes to haunt the community that sold her into slavery or that murdered her to prevent her from being sold into slavery. The lack of such a substantive and dynamic representation of slavery in West African literature is what Murphy laments about.

In chapter five of her book entitled "The Curse of Constant Remembrance: The Belated Trauma of the Slave Trade in Ayi Kwei Armah's Fragments," Murphy deconstructs how Armah's narrative of slavery fits into a "coded discourse" built around metaphors that fall into the category of a sort of "symbolic annihilation". This blackwashing of slavery in West African literature is all the more surprising as literature is the most appropriate venue to raise the issue of slavery and all the questions it entails. Indeed, literature, in opposition to history, is the most suitable medium to relate wounded histories. In this respect, Nancy Peterson writes in *Against Amnesia*: "Wounded histories are written as literature, or fiction, and not as history, for only literature in our culture is allowed the narrative flexibility and the suspension of disbelief that are crucial to the telling of these histories." (p. 7) Drawing on Woodard and Murphy's work, we can infer that the sentimental attachments to historical injury of slavery of the West Africans and African Americans diverge as reflected in their slave narratives. The continental Africans are reluctant to engage a sincere debate about slavery in their literature let alone in their history books where the repercussions are direct since history does not allow room for the suspension of disbelief. The continental African's memory of slavery is deflected away from its historicity. Much the same is true with the African slave forts. Instead of becoming historical edifices that are meant to render the highest truth about the past, and in so doing restore the historicity, slave forts are turned into mere business tourist sites. Woodard draws our attention to this fact in these terms: "Given the explosion in heritage tourism in Africa, or what Marita Sturken refers to as "trauma tourism," slave forts may well override Paul Gilroy's slave ship as microcosmic rallying symbol for dispersed slave descendants." (p. 29) This "trauma tourism" strips the slave fort of its historical symbolism. The slave fort becomes then a means through which the regional Africans can find a source of livelihood. The policy implication of this reality deserves to be analyzed.

CODA

A "flash" moment reading of the prevalence of "trauma tourism" in West Africa

The Senegalese slave fort, Gorée, is located in a peninsula, deprived of factories or major companies where the youth can work and make money. The only activities available to them are fishing and tourism. And since fishing has become unproductive due to a pareto-efficient allocation of resources, among others, the youth of Gorée, like the other youth in the coastal regions of Senegal, have decided to venture illegal emigration. Good public policy has to improve the overall welfare of society. But the allocation of resources being always pareto-efficient, principally being unable to make the youth well off. The latter represent the vast majority of the population. Just the youth under 20 represent 55% of the population according to the 2019 data survey by ANSD (Agence Nationale de la Statistique et de la Démographie). However, we need to concede that "Public policy is whatever governments choose to do or not do, that is to say government action and inaction'' (p. 12) as Dye puts it. Inaction, too, as Dye argues, refers to situations in which policymakers 'do nothing' about a societal issue. This policy of 'do nothing' has encouraged the youth to venture illegal emigration.

The Senegalese filmmaker Moussa Séne Absa documents this phenomenon in his 2010 film *Yoole*. Moussa Séne Absa's *Yoole* shows that there is a sort of reversed slavery or neo-slavery in which it is poverty that drives the vigorous African youth to venture the Atlantic Ocean for Europe.

Also, in their essay "L'émigration clandestine sénégalaise" (or Senegalese illegal emigration) Cheikh Oumar Ba and Alfred Iniss Ndiaye analyze the social and political motives and consequences of illegal emigration. Drawing on the socio-economic senegalese context, they define illegal emigration in these terms:

> Elle devient aussi une migration d'espoir. Le mot « clandestin » désigne aujourd'hui au Sénégal les personnes qui empruntent illégalement des pirogues pour se rendre en Europe. Le clandestin est celui qui brave la mer, la faim et la soif, celui qui risque sa vie pour atteindre un objectif noble, celui d'accéder au marché du travail et de chercher à sortir sa famille de la pauvreté. (p. 2)

It is also becoming a migration of hope. The word "clandestine" today in Senegal refers to people who illegally borrow canoes to get to Europe. The illegal is the one who braves the sea, hunger and thirst, the one who risks his or her life to achieve a noble goal, that of accessing the labor market and seeking to lift his or her family out of poverty. (My translation)

Cheikh Oumar Ba and Alfred Iniss Ndiaye relate the testimony of a young Senegalese candidate for illegal emigration:

> Un jeune confiait: « en me lançant dans la migration clandestine, j'ai 50% de chance de mourir dans le désert ou dans l'Océan et 50% d'atteindre mon objectif. Or, en restant au pays, je suis presque sûr à 100% de mourir à petit feu. » (p. 6)

A young man confided: "By embarking on illegal migration, I have a 50% chance of dying in the desert or in the ocean and 50% chance of reaching my goal. However, by staying in the country, I am almost 100% sure that I will die slowly. (My translation)

Drawing on the "flash" moment concept, I read these waves of illegal emigrations from West Africa as a sort of post-modern slavery or reversed slavery that engages directly with modern African history. And in so doing, they speak to the existing literature on history, neo-slavery, human trafficking, memory, and migrations. The failure of current West African policy makers and leaders to provide employment to their youth has created unprecedented socio-economic and political circumstances.

Here again, I can turn to art to better articulate this situation. Richard Wright's following poem, extracted from his book *Black Boy*, where he writes down his own migration from the North to the South can help apprehend the pain, the dilemma, and the vague hope of finding prosperity elsewhere of the illegal West African emigrants:

> I was leaving the South
> To fling myself into the unknown...
> I was taking a part of the South
> To transplant in alien soil,
> To see if it could grow differently,
> It it could drink of new and cool rains,

> Bend in strange winds,
> Respond to the warmth of other suns
> And, perhaps, to bloom.

The migration that Richard Wright describes here is not cross national but it helps a lot in understanding the waves of the West African illegal youth emigration. Like Wright's migration which is supposed to mark the end of an epoch of suffering, incarceration and lack of opportunities, the West African young illegal emigrant runs away from his home country for the similar reasons. Therefore, the North like Europe becomes the magnet that attracts the desperate people. The South has set up an oppressive system that prevents the blacks from blooming. In the same vein, the chronic failure of the West African leaders to provide opportunities for the youth has stifled the patriotism of the latter. They don't see themselves benefitting from the huge wealth of the continent's resources. The resources are used, as it has been in the past, to serve those outside of the continent. That's why post-colonial African literature is a literature of disillusionment that focuses on the mal governance and its repercussions on the continent.

Indeed, contemporary post-colonial African literature sees the current West African rulers as neo-colonizers, modern slave traders. Armah in his satirical novel *The Beautiful Ones Are Not Yet Born* compares in a poignant passage the present African leaders to the ancient African kings who enrich themselves by selling their own people. Here runs the passage: "And yet these were the socialists of Africa, fat, perfumed, soft with the ancestral softness of chiefs who had sold their people and are celestially happy with the fruits of the trade." (p.131) Post-colonial African literature is specially a literature of disillusionment. The newly independent African people soon realize that their own fellow countrymen who replace the white colonizers are not that different from their new leaders; and to some extent the new leaders are worse. In other words, regardless of the big change that happened- a shift from colonization, dependency to independence, self-governance - the same system remains. In other words, if in precolonial or colonial Africa there was a commodification of human beings, now there is commodification of the public resources. Murphy, in analyzing the representation of slavery in Armah's fiction, draws our attention to this fact:

> Ayi Kwei Armah has explicitly confronted the slave trade in his fiction more than any other West African writer of the twentieth

century. *Two Thousand Seasons*, perhaps his most historically driven novel, tells the story of a collective pan-African response to centuries of oppression at the hands of "white destroyers" who come from the desert and then from the ocean. Following an undeniably loose historical trajectory of African migrations that were at times threatened by and at times prompted by the trans-Saharan and the transatlantic slave trades, the novel utilizes the form of the written-oral epic to depict the heroic struggle of a small collective of Africans who refused to resign themselves to white power. A first-person plural "we" narrator strives to maintain a sense of "the way" - Armah's name for an African traditional culture and ethic that can guide African people out of domination by white destroyers and the tyranny of their "parasites," Africans who fed off the African community in order to access white power. (p. 25-26)

Murphy provides here an opportunity for the reader of Armah's text to see the complicated and overlapping processes through which there is no rupture in Africa's interaction with the rest of the world, on the one hand, and in the way in which the Africans have been treated by both the "white destroyers" or their "parasites" on the other hand. Murphy categories Armah's fiction as "a narrative of palimpsestic oppressions" (p. 28) that lays bare the oppression that Africa has been a victim of for debates. Armah takes on an authorial responsibility to act, like Toni Morrison, as both historian and writer. Therefore, literature like history or anthropology can function as a medium through which the trauma of a community and its effects can be grasped. Armah's text shows that African history is not linear since linearity implies progress. In this respect, Armah's text engages with Ellison's *Invisible Man*. Armah sets the president's abode in the former slave castle so as to show that African history will always boomerang, letting the people incapable of changing its course.

The repressed memory of slavery by some Africans of the diaspora:

In "African modes of Self-Writing," Achille Mbembe informs us that in some parts of the New World, the descendants of African slaves repress their memory of slavery. In this respect, Mbembe writes:

> In certain parts of the New World, the memory of slavery is consciously repressed by the descendants of African slaves. The tragedy at the origin of the drama that constitutes their existence in the present is constantly denied. Because it is denied, this tragedy can never produce, by itself, any law or foundation. To be sure, this denial is not equivalent to forgetting as such. It is simultaneously a refusal to acknowledge one's ancestry and a refusal to remember an act that arouses feelings of shame. Under such conditions, the priority is not really to re-establish contact with oneself and with one's origins. Neither is it a question of restoring a full and positive relationship to oneself, since this self has been humiliated beyond any limit. The narrative of slavery having been condemned to be elliptical, a sort of ghost persecutes and haunts the subject and inscribes on his unconscious the dead body of a way of speaking that must be constantly repressed. For in order to exist in the present, it is considered necessary to forget the name of the father in the very act by which one claims to ask the question of the origin and of filiation. This is, notably, the case in the Antilles. (p. 20)

The question we may then ask is such a repression of memory healing? And what kind of identity comes out of such a repression? The fictional work of Morrison *Paradise* provides some answers to these questions particularly the discussion between Patricia and Reverent Misner regarding the Negro history curriculum. But before coming to the discussion between Patricia and Reverent Misner related to the Negro history curriculum, let us set the context. Patricia has a history project that she holds dear and near. Through Patricia's history project, Morrison provides answers to the questions of who is naming or recording history and also what makes a history legitimate or illegitimate. These themes are inextricably interdependent.

Patricia's history project consists in writing down the genealogies of each family in the town Ruby, an all-black run town. Let us just start by quoting this long passage that lays out Patricia's history project (and at the same time, we will highlight some key sentences):

> Pat climbed the stairs to her bedroom and decided to while away the rest of the evening on her history project but was nothing of the sort now. It began as a gift to the citizens of Ruby -- a collection of family trees; the genealogies of each of the fifteen families. *Upside-down*

trees, the trunks sticking in the air, the branches sloping down. When the trees were completed, she had begun to supplement the branches of who begot whom with notes: what work they did, for example, where they lived, to what church they belonged. Some of the nicer touches ("Was Missy Rivers, wife of Thomas Blackhorse, born near the Mississippi River? Her name seems to suggest...") *she had gleaned from her students' autobiographical compositions.* Not anymore. Parents complained about their children being asked to gossip, to divulge what could be private information, secrets, even. After that most of her notes came from talking to people, asking to see Bibles and examining church records. *Things got out of hands when she asked to see letters and marriage certificates.* The women narrowed their eyes before smiling and offering to freshen her coffee. Invisible doors closed, and the conversation turned to weather. But she didn't want or need any further research. The trees still required occasional alterations - births, marriages, deaths - but her interest in the supplementary notes increased as the notes did, and she gave up all pretense to objective comments. The project became unfit for any eyes except her own. It had reached the point where the small *m* period was a joke, a dream, a violation of law that had her biting her thumbnail in frustration. *Who were these women who, like her mother, had only one name? Celeste, Olive, Sorrow, Ivlin, Pansy.* Who were these women with generalized names? Brown, Smith, Rivers, Stone, Jones. Women whose identity rested on the men they married --- if marriage applied a Morgan, a Flood, a Blackhorse, a Poole, a Fleetwood. Dovey had let her have the Morgan Bible for weeks, but it was the twenty minutes she spent looking at the Blackhorse Bible that convinced her that a new species of tree would be needed to go further, to record accurately the relationship among the fifteen families of Ruby, their ancestors in Haven and, further back, in Mississippi and Louisiana. A voluntary act to fill empty hours had become intensive labor streaked with the bad feelings that ride the skin like pollen when too much about one's neighbors is known. *The town's official story elaborated from pulpits, in Sunday school classes and ceremony speeches, had a sturdy public life.* Any footnotes, crevices or questions to be put took keen imagination and the persistence of a mind uncomfortable with oral histories. *Pat had wanted proof in documents where possible to match stories, and where proof was available she interpreted - freely but, she thought, insightfully because she alone had the required emotional distance.* She alone would figure out why a line was drawn through Ethan Blackhorse's name in the Blackhorse Bible and what the heavy ink blot hid next to Zechariah's name in the Morgan Bible. *Her father told her things, but he refused to talk about other things.* Girlfriends like Kate and Anna were open, but older women - Dovey, Soane, Lone, DuPres, - hinted the most while saying the least. "Oh, I think those brothers had a disagreement of some kind." That's all Soane would say about crossed-out names of her great uncle. And not another word. (187-189) (emphasis added)

This passage that captures Patricia's history project is very significant since it raises important questions, such as can we write down history without any dose of subjectivity? And if we add or interpret some elements under whose eyes is this version of history legitimate? And can we recover a history when some elements are missing? Or when the witnesses are gone or reluctant to speak up? And what is the instrument that allows us to distinguish "official history, story" from "oral histories, stories"? Based on these questions that Patricia tries to provide an answer, we can argue that Patricia's history project is in fact Morrison's. Morrison discusses here the question of what and who legitimizes a history. The passage that describes Patricia's history project informs us that Patricia's history project is not deemed legitimate in the eyes of many people in Ruby. A missing thread in the string of questions raised in the quoted passage of Patricia's history project is: Is forgetting about the past healing or redeeming? *Beloved* answers this question through the ghost Beloved that comes to haunt the present. Part of Ellison's narrative tackles this question. Ellison's answer to this question is that *"...history was not a reasonable citizen, but a madman full of paranoid guile..."* (441) To him, history can't be rationalized or contained. That is to say, history always circles back, and you can't forget it nor wipe it out. And, as far as Morrison is concerned, the past is in the present, meaning the present bears marks of absences, silences, and ellipses that make the past dog the present. For example, Patricia's history project has instances that illustrate how the present contains the past. Patricia asks when she encounters these elliptical names, *"Who were these women who, like her mother, had only one name? Celeste, Olive, Sorrow, Ivlin, Pansy."* (187) It is these ellipses and silences which you can't hide nor silence that blends the past with the present. And in

Beloved, the same elliptical names are encountered. Paul D Garner, Paul F Garner, Paul A Garner ect. Ellipses are meaningful only to those who can grasp what's left out. Morrison underscores the significance of ellipses as she calls Patricia Pat almost throughout the chapter "Patricia". The life of the inhabitants of Ruby is dogged by these ellipses that people pretend to ignore while being hyper-conscious that they are hanging over their heads, ready to crash them if they speak too much or open the 'invisible doors'. Patricia informs us that her father says least than he knows so do the elder women, "*Her father told her things, but he refused to talk about other things. Girlfriends like Kate and Anna were open, but older women - Dovey, Soane, Lone, DuPres, -- hinted the most while saying the least..*" (189) Speaking too much or opening the 'invisible doors' opens up the wounds of the history. Indeed, as Jameson reminds us in *The Political Unconscious*, "history is what hurts". History is indeed, for Ellison and Morrison's characters, a long string of atrocities, disappointments, betrayal, and retroversions (turning back or resurfacing). To avoid the stigmas and effects of history to resurface, Patricia's father and the elder women in Ruby refuse to speak out. Each of the genealogy question that Patricia asks is a history that conjures a historian or historiographer. But Patricia's father and the elder women of Ruby don't want to act as historians or historiographers. They are barely acting as oral historians. Morrison equates this feigned amnesia of the past with some sort of death for the whole community of Ruby. This forced or feigned amnesia is not healing at all; it causes a "rewound," a term I coined in juxtaposition with Morrison's neologism "rememory." "Rewound" is a wound that refuses to heal. This feigned amnesia of the past of the inhabitants of Ruby captures the refusal of the Antilles to embrace their ancestor. Therefore, to paraphrase Mbembe's argument in the quotation opening this section, we can argue that the same refusal of Africans to acknowledge their answerability in the slave trade because it arouses feelings of shame and powerlessness is akin to the refusal of the Antilles to embrace an ancestry who awakens the same feelings.

In discussing the Negro history curriculum, about the education of black teenagers, with Reverent Richard Misner, the latter says to Patricia, "*If you cut yourself off from the roots, you'll wither. Roots that ignore the branches turn into termite dust.*" (209) Patricia wants to dig up the history of Ruby, and rewrite it without any subjectivity. And yet, there is a part of her own history that she doesn't want to dig up, identify with, or understand. Patricia, as a history recorder, wants to recover only the side of history that means something to her. As she says in her dialogue with Reverent Richard Misner: "Pat," he (Reverent

Richard Misner) said with mild surprise. *"You despise Africa." "No," I don't. It just doesn't mean something to me."* (209) The reader is shocked by Patricia's response about Africa. How can she recover the history of her community, Ruby, if she overlooks the origin of their history? Patricia like the dominant national narrative or historiography is being selective. Reverent Richard Misner replies to Patricia in this passage:

> "Africa is our home, Pat, whether you like it or not...
> "We live in the world, Pat. The whole world. Separating us, isolating us - that has always been their weapon. Isolation kills generations. It has no future." (210)

Reverent Richard Misner's argument that to ignore the past creates a vacuum that kills generations connects well with the idea that forgetting the past leads to a "rewound." A vacuum is a void in the space, and a wound is a void in the body, and a "rewound" is a regeneracy of a healing wound. In both case scenarios, there's a fracture, something missing, or mal functioning. Patricia, unlike Reverent Richard Misner, can't see this void if Africa is erased from the African-American history.

Patricia can't draw a connection with a distant homeland that her great grandparents are said to be snatched from if she hadn't been taught about that homeland. Africa has been missing in US history curriculum. Africa has been omitted that's what Reverent Richard Misner alludes to when he says, *"Separating us, isolating us - that has always been their weapon"* (210). To break this vicious cycle of isolation, Reverent Richard Misner talks to Patricia into including Africa into the curriculum so that the current and future generations of black teenagers won't feel the same home-rejection that infects Patricia. In another passage, Reverent Richard Misner insists on the significance of home:

> "This is their home; mine too. Home is not a little thing."
> "I'm not saying it is. But can't you even imagine what it must feel like to have a home. Not some fortress you bought and built up and have to keep everybody locked in or out. A real home. Not some place you went to and invaded and slaughtered people to get. Not some place you claimed, snatched because you got the guns. Not some place you stole from the people living there, but your own home, where if you go back past your great-great- grandparents, past theirs, and theirs,

past the whole of Western history, past the beginning of organized knowledge, past pyramids and poison bows, on back to when rain was new, before plants forgot they could sing and birds thought they were fish, back when God said Good! Good! - there, right there where you know your own people were born and lived and died. Imagine that, Pat. That place. Who was God talking to if not to my people living in my home." (213)

Yet, despite Reverent Misner's insistence on home, Patricia can't seize the importance of home. Breaking the vicious cycle of isolation that Patricia is bundled up is not easy. Patricia is piecing together historical documents so as to understand the history of Ruby, but the big piece of the puzzle that links her and the Ruby inhabitants to their origin is missing. This explains why after compiling and writing her history compendium she burns it. She doesn't know what to make of it not because her history book is not legitimate before the eyes of the Ruby community, but because the missing bridge that would connect the dots, and make the project complete and meaningful is home: Africa. In other words, Africa is the dot linking home to the transplanted home. Patricia is not conscious of this missing bridge. She doesn't know much about Africa and is not interested in knowing about it, let alone let her students study Africa. About including Africa into the curriculum, she says, "*I don't limit anything. I just don't believe some stupid devotion to a foreign country - and Africa is a foreign country, in fact it's fifty foreign countries - is a solution for these kids.*" (210) Patricia's stance about history matches that of diaspora slave descendants of the Antilles that Mbembe describes as people who utterly reject their origin.

Patricia lacks a substantial knowledge about Africa as she raises one question that puzzles both the reader and Reverent Richard Misner. Her question can be paraphrased as such, "Are there other homes than Africa?" As she puts it:

I'm really not interested, Richard. You want some foreign Negroes to identify with, why not South America? Or Germany, for that matter. They have some brown babies over there you could have a good time connecting with. Or is it just some kind of past with no slavery in it you're looking for?" (210)

Patricia's claim that there may be a home or another home other than Africa explains why she is completely lost to the point of burning her history book. There is no referent or starting point at all for her. And almost all of Reverent

Richard Misner's answers to Patricia's questions point to the starting point, the referent, as his reply to Patricia's claim that there are probably other homes than Africa illustrates, "*You're wrong, and if that's your field you're plowing wet. Slavery is our past. Nothing can change that, certainly not Africa.*" (210) Morrison's description of Patricia's stand to history befits the denial of diaspora slave descendants of the Antilles (West Indies). Such a repression of memory and history is not healing at all. It leaves the diaspora slave descendants more disoriented. Maybe that's why Patricia ends up burning her history project. But what does Patricia's burning of her history project mean other than the fact that there is a crucial missing dot? The project is incomplete, but it has many an accurate information. Does this mean that only a history that is complete and accurate deserve to be archived? Can't another historian finish up the project? When we try to answer these questions within the framework of the suppression of home of diaspora slave descendants of the Antilles, it becomes clear that Morrison grounds Africa as a root or foundation from which grows the various diaspora slave descendants, including the Antilles for better or worse. That's why, Morrison let Reverent Richard Misner insist that "*Slavery is our past. Nothing can change that, certainly not Africa.*" (210) In other words, Reverent Richard Misner is telling to Patricia that Africa is like the North Star that assisted runaway-slaves find their direction to freedom. Africa is such a North Star without which the African diaspora lose a sense of direction. And as Invisible Man informs us in the epilogue, "Perhaps to lose a sense of *where* you are implies the danger of losing a sense of *who* you are. That must be it, I thought- to lose your direction is to lose your face" (p. 577)

Daniel Maragnes, in his essay "Identité et le désastre" where he analyzes the repression of memory of the Antilles and at the same time compares the Jewish and Black diaspora, he describes the Patricia-like suppression of memory in the Antilles in this passage:

> Rien de semblable aux Antilles. Tout se passe véritablement comme si s'effectuait un mouvement parfaitement inverse, posant la mémoire dans les marges même de l'existence, comme son exclue. La fondation esclavagiste est ainsi proprement niée, la mémoire du drame constitutif exactement perdue. (p. 2)

Nothing much like the Antilles (West Indies). Everything really happens as if a perfectly reverse movement was taking place, placing memory on the very margins of existence, as its outcast. The slavery foundation is thus properly denied, and the memory of the constitutive drama exactly lost. (My translation)

As Daniel Maragnes highlights here the Antilles put the memory of slavery at the margins. Such a denial of one's ancestry which tends to render the origin untraceable leads Maragnes to ask the questions why does slavery and its terrible pangs not illuminate the present of the communities that were formed, woven by them? He explains that this is in part due to the fact that contrary to the Jewish diaspora which is bound together by a nationhood and a book, the African diaspora are really diverse and at times divided against themselves. Daniel Maragnes sums up the contrast between the Jewish and Black diaspora in these terms:

> La sortie d'Egypte est une positivité pour la fondation juive, cette libération de Pharaon qui va fonder un peuple. La « sortie d'Afrique » des esclaves noirs est un mouvement parfaitement inverse où un nouveau peuple se fonde dans l'histoire silencieuse des cales. (p. 2)

The exit from Egypt is a positivity for the Jewish foundation, this liberation from Pharaoh which will result in the birth of a people. The "exit from Africa" of the black slaves is a completely opposite movement where a new people is founded in the silent history of the holds. (My translation)

As Maragnes implies here the division of black diaspora results in "the silent history of the holds". The suppression of memory of slavery of the Antilles falls into this category of "the silent history of the holds". Much the same is true with the muted rationales that have engendered the difference in the sentimental attachments to historical injury of slavery among the diaspora community. Therefore, we can elaborate on Maragnes' argument that the divisive dispersion of the black diaspora comes first from the place where slaves were kept prior to deportation, I mean slave forts. Who brought them there? And atrocities mental or physical did they go through? With the slave forts in West Africa (much like the ones in Brazil), it becomes always impossible to reconstitute the historical truth. Woodard frames this issue around the authenticity of slave sites.

Hubert Gerbeau, in *Les Esclaves noirs: Pour une histoire du silence*, articulates much like Maragnes and Woodard that there is a powerful discourse of silence around which the history of slavery is built. There is a silence of the slave, and a silence on the slave. Morrison to break these silences on and of the slave invents a narrative in which the atrocities of history are embodied by the child ghost, what Adam Z. Newton calls "metempyschosis" (100), a sort of reincarnation. In the midst of all these silences around slavery that these authors raise, it is not surprising that the Antilles, unable to break through this opacity of silence and thereafter build the obvious clarity of a lineage, decide, like Patricia, to ignore their ancestry. But the politico-ethical and historical imperatives demand that these silences be broken. In Morrison's narrative, Patricia's rejection of her ancestry leads her to be lost to the point of burning her book. And in the case of the Antilles, it thickens the shadowy zone of silence among the Africans of the diaspora and the continental Africans. This means that the collective memory of slavery can't serve as a particular mobilizing criterion for the Black diaspora. Then racial and political consciousness will not be identical across the Black diaspora. It is also necessary to underline that racial and political consciousness are not identical within the continent either.

Mbembe's essay raises also the issues of democratization and nation building in Africa. As he points out, tribes in Africa are an otherizing factor. Instead of enabling social and political inclusion, tribal identity becomes discriminatory. This is what Mbembe calls "customary identity." (p. 8) The recent ethnic conflicts in Mali (I am alluding to the conflicts between ethnic Dogon, traditionally farmers, and Fulani or Peulh, semi-nomadic herders on June 9, 2019) drives us to fear tribal affiliations since they trump democratic and republican foundations. They jeopardize the process of nation building and democratization. The ethnic conflicts in Mali are caused by but "a racialization of the nation and the nationalization of the race" to use Mbembe's phrase (p. 13). But it would be more accurate to say a tribalization of the nation and the nationalization of the tribe. A good example here is the last presidential election in Senegal (elections held in Senegal on 24 February 2019) where the candidate Ousmane Sonko and incumbent president Macky Sall who have a clear tribal or ethnic identity have won massively in the regions where their respective ethnic groups reside. Tribal or ethnic identity becomes then the basic for social and political solidarity. Yet, if Africa, as a continent, is defined to be heterogeneous, and that heterogeneity lacks a unifying identity, then all the nation building endeavors as well as the continental projects of integration are put in peril. Mbembe proposes a revisionist narrative that invites us to clarify and modify the principles of unity and identity in Africa. If racial identity is tribalized, then, how can there be a pan-African nation, or the United States of Africa. In other words, can there be *E pluribus Unum* in the national and continental level if this tribalized division prevails? This question is worth asking since the Other who played on this division to inflict slavery and colonization on us will use it again to further divide and dominate us. And ironically, it is no surprise that the Jihadists are playing on this difference to take control of Sub-Saharan Africa. Esha Sarai, in "Ethnic Conflicts in Mali Exacerbated by Extremist Presence," makes a thorough analysis of this new phenomenon. Esha Sarai's argument coheres with Mbembe's claim that "the colonial state used custom - that is, the principle of difference and the refusal of alterity - as a mode of government in itself" (p. 8) This concern is raised by Mahmood Mamdani, in *Citizen and Subject: Contemporary Africa and the Legacy of Late Colonialism*. Mamdani, in analyzing the obstacles to democratization in post-independence Africa, identifies tribal based governance as a legacy of colonialism that Africans have to reform.

On balance, faced with all this complex pending inner problems, how can Africa reach out to the black diasporic subject and pay the debt she owes him or her. My contention here is that before curing the historical injury that Africa has inflicted on the diasporic subject, Africans have to rethink their concept of alterity and plurality within the continent since "racial and territorial authenticity are conflated, and Africa becomes the country of black people. At the same time, everything that is not black is out of place, and thus cannot claim any sort of Africanity." (p.14) as Mbembe informs us. We have to come to terms if what defines Africaness or Africanity within the continent before reaching out to the diasporic subject. To do so, tribal or ethnic affiliations have to be put at the rear back. Self-governance, development, democracy, and regional integration can only exist if there is an *E pluribus Unum* in the national and continental level. Ellison in his second novel *Juneteenth* brings some answers to these questions about nation building and embracing plurality that could aptly fit into the African context.

In Senator Sunraider's speech, he poses the set of contradictions that are inherent in the American democracy. He raises three questions that the U.S., as a socio-political ideology, must face in its nation building process. The address of the Senator which starts in chapter two lays out the major themes that are developed further in the narrative. In other words, in terms of narrative structure, the address of the Senator corresponds to the preparation phase in the narrative framework. The senator formulates the three nation-building questions and tries at the same time to provide an answer to them in these terms:

> "I need not remind you that I am neither seer nor prophet," he went on, "but history has put to us three fatal questions, has written them across our sky in accents of accusation. They are, How can the many be as one? How can the future deny the past? And How can the light deny the dark? The answer to the first is: Through a balanced consciousness of unity in diversity and diversity in unity, through a willed and *conscious* balance --- that is the key phrase, so easy to say yet so difficult to maintain.
>
> "For the second, the answer lies in remembering that, given the nature of our wisdom, of our covenant, to remember is to forget and to forget is to remember selectively, creatively! Yes, and let us remember that in this land to create is to destroy, and to destroy --- if we will it so and *make* it so, if we pay our proper respect to remembered but rejected things --- is to make manifest our lovely dream of progressive idealism.
>
> "And how can light deny the dark? Why, by seeking ever the darkness in lightness and lightness in darkness. As we incorporate and humanize nature we filter and blend the spectrum, we exalt and we anguish, we order the world. (19)

These thorny questions that the Senator articulates here are called further down in his address "*our national ambiguities.*" These national ambiguities that Ellison endeavors to resolve through his fiction cohere with the challenges of nation building and democratization in Africa, in particular West Africa. As the Senator contends, creating "a balanced consciousness of unity in diversity and diversity in unity" is the first stage in the nation building process of a racially or tribally diverse citizenry. But as he admits implementing the policies that will tear down the national ambiguities are very demanding. Indeed, implementing such policies are not just demanding but also, they are not an overnight enterprise. Moreover, as the Senator suggests, to build this cohesive nation, we have to give due consideration to the past: to remember or to forget selectively. And slavery falls into the Africans' national and continental ambiguities that needs to be remembered selectively.

Slavery's answerability represented in African American literature:

When discussing the authenticity of West African slave forts, Woodard highlights the failure of traditional historical archival to render the historical truth. In other words, the real historical questions about the slave forts are deflected. She relates such a deflection in this passage:

The unanswered questions do not so much entail whether the Portuguese, Dutch, or English built or managed the fort. Instead, those in the Indigenous population simply demand to know what happened to their ancestors who disappear from local villages during the slave trade. Those African families whose loved ones were seized and taken to those forts wistfully pondered what atrocities occurred inside the huge stone monster by the sea where people arrived and departed across the Atlantic in the Middle Passage, and never returned. (p. 32)

One crucial question left out by Woodard in her string of questions is who seized and took those African families to the slave forts. Ironically, this omission mimics the way historians lower the volume on controversial debates about the who were involved in seizing and taking those African families to the forts. And further down in the same passage, Woodard writes "But as material archive and visual premier marker, the House of Slaves conveys the past through an "authorized" imperial lens and a counterhistorical intervention" (p. 32) This passage draws out our attention to the different ideologies governing slave sites. Because of these different ideologies governing slave sites, the issues of shared responsibility of slavery can't be openly discussed. Yet African American literature alludes to this thorny issue. *Invisible Man* deals with this issue metaphorically.

In chapter 2O, Tod Clifton is portrayed selling Sambo dolls. And Sambo doll dates back to the time of slavery and it denotes a docile and loyal slave. So, as I read the narrative, Tod Clifton's selling of Sambo dolls alludes directly to this thorny problem. The reader is appalled by Tod Clifton's act. This allusion is made more explicit when the narrator comments that, "*there's no licence for little sambo*" (433), meaning that to sell a little Sambo, you don't need a license or any legal document. It is clear that Ellison metaphorizes here an instance of commodification of human beings. In the Tod Clifton scene, Tod Clifton sings a jingle while making the dolls dance, and the audience is there staring; Invisible Man is appalled by Tod Clifton's act and he calls him traitor. The jingle runs like this:

> *Shake it up! Shake ip up!*
> *He is Sambo, the dancing doll, ladies and gentlemen.*
> *Shake him, stretch him by the neck and set him down,*
> *-He'll do the rest. Yes!*
> *He'll make you laugh, he'll make you sign, si-gh.*
> *He'll make you want to dance, and dance---*
> *Here you are, ladies and gentlemen, Sambo,*
> *The dancing doll.*
> *Buy one for your baby. Take him to your girlfriend and she'll love you,*
> *Loove you!*
> *He'll keep you entertained. He'll make you weep sweet---*
> *Tears from laughing.*
> *Shake him, shake him, you cannot break him*
> *For he's Sambo, the dancing, Sambo, the prancing,*
> *Sambo the entertaining, Sambo Boogie Woogie paper doll.*
> *And all for twenty-five cents, the quarter part of a dollar... (326)*

In analyzing the social and political functions of metaphors in literary work, Murphy articulates that "The very root of the word *metaphor* is linked to the notion of transfer. Metaphor carries and transports our often nearly unspeakable meanings for us; it transfers our values, concerns, fears, and recollections to others." (p. 9) Reading the Sambo doll scene in the light of Murphy's quotation makes first the Samdo dolls stand for mere cultural survival forms. Hence by selling them Clifton gets rid of his memories about Africa. In other words, Clifton expresses his desire not to retain any connection with Africa or the slave past in America. The dolls may symbolize, too, Clifton's own shackling, metaphorically, by the dominant cultural establishment as Greene argues. The second reading of the Sambo doll scene in the light of Murphy's quotation reveals a metaphorized commodification of human beings. Indeed, one point that Murphy does not raise is her analysis of metaphors is that metaphors are opaque and because of this opacity they offer a plethora of interpretations. That's why the Sambo dolls have been interpreted differently by literary critics.

In this respect, Nadel, in *Invisible Criticism*, writes, "Unclear about Clifton's motives, the interpreters reach non-consensus about what his relationship to the dolls signifies" (p. 65) Yet if we make a deconstructive characterization of Clifton, it becomes clear that Clifton stands for the absent who is omnipresent. He is an embodied legend. Nadel introduces Clifton in these terms:

> Although Clifton appears in two chapters (three if we count his funeral), his name is mentioned in each of the nine chapters from the point of his introduction through the epilogue; in all, it is mentioned well over 150 times. Clifton's behavior, moreover leaves much to be explained. We know almost nothing about his origins, we don't know why he disappears or why he chooses to reappear selling Sambo dolls. (p. 64)

What Nadel does not elaborate on is that Clifton's appearance in the text aggregates to roughly 200 times which corresponds to the time span of the slave trade (200 years), which amounts also to two centuries, metaphorizing the two chapters in which Clifton takes part. All these elements with which Clifton is woven turns him into a very enigmatic and opaque figure that literary critics have yet to pierce. Yet, even though Ellison structures the narrative in such a way that it is not easy to pin down Clifton, his selling of Sambo dolls and the fact that Invisible Man distances himself from him shows someone who has fallen from grace to grass. It is important to point out that in some passages of the text Tod Clifton is referred to as "a chief, a black king" (p. 281) Also Nadel informs us that "Clifton's ostensibly nonhistorical act is recorded in police records and newspapers, and its effects riots similarly in historical documents." (p. 66) The fact that Clifton's act is seemingly recorded in historical document brings up more textual evidence that Ellison deals with a complex historical event that metaphors only can convey since, as Murphy contends, "Metaphors package a traumatic past in a way that is digestible, communicable, and comprehensible. They turn literal pain into images that transmit the memory of suffering through the generations" (p. 21)

Nadel personally reads the Sambo scene as a passage about betrayal (involving the betrayed and betrayer) "resiliency and emptiness, deity and fallen angel, humanity and machinization" (77). Nadel further writes, "In other words, the Sambo dolls suggest infinite possibilities and show that the meaning of a black image depends upon its interpreters, just like the meaning of betrayal depends on one's loyalties" (77). Nadel's claim that his passage revolves around a narrative of betrayal and fallen angel makes sense. Indeed, later by the end of the chapter, when Invisible Man meditates on Tod Clifton's act, he asks why Tod Clifton has chosen to *"fall outside of history"* (434). Invisible Man is overwhelmed by a strong feeling of guilt and cowardice. He views Tod Clifton as a black man, "a chief, a black king", who has just unmade history. Ironically, right after his act, Clifton is murdered by a white policeman for selling sambo dolls as if to efface his crime. This technique of effacement implies that there are many innuendoes and censored arguments buried in the text. The narrative structure stands between two complementary poles of censorship and self-censorship, which mirrors perfectly the problematic of history writing and archivization. History writing is always a matter of conflicting evidence, and thereby next to the truth there is always some retention of information, fabulation, alteration, and falsehood. Archivization proceeds the same way. Archivization is never neutral but it rather fits into a particular and suitable narrative. Quoting Derrida, Crownshaw defines archivization as "… consignation which aims to coordinate a single corpus, in a system in which all the elements articulate the unity of an ideal configuration […] without any heterogeneity.'' (p. 219)

    The heterogeneous body that the archivist has to piece together into an "ideal configuration" deflects the archival narrative away from the historical truth. The archival narrative is an incomplete account of history. This incomplete account of history is not possible without some censorship or self-censorship. By presenting the Clifton scene in such a way it withstands interpretation, Ellison deploys an archivization narrative structure that censors itself, saying least than it knows as if it does not want to be answerable or liable to blame. This technique of censorship is even extended to the characters. Invisible Man as one of the witnesses of Clifton's act tries his most to erase the scene out of his mind. Even the policeman who murders Clifton disappeared in the text, he is no longer mentioned. In other words, Clifton and his act are not claimed like Morrison's Beloved. Speaking about Beloved, Morrison writes: "Disremembered and unaccounted for, she cannot be lost because no one is looking for her, and even if they were, how can they call her if they don't know her name? Although she has claim, she is not cl aimed." (323) Morrison poses here the question of answerability regarding slavery. Beloved is not claimed because no one wants to take up that responsibility. Answerability entails always guilt. A guilt that the bystanders, victims, and perpetrators try to silence that is why the narrative structure has tactfully let the murder of Clifton give so much sound and fury that the narration shifts radically its focus onto the black and white difficult cohabitation. Through Tod Clifton's murder, Ellison reveals how, like a heritage, the implications of the past still determine the relationship between the black and white communities. Clifton's chapter concludes with the race riot.

Also, the thorny issues of slavery's answerability that Ellison attempts to fictionalize is being raised in the current African academic debate about slavery. The Senegalese historian, Ibrahima Thioub argues that Africans were greatly involved in the gathering and selling of slaves. Ibrahima Thioub makes that claim in an interview with Camille Bauer reported by the French newspaper *Parti de Gauche Midi* (January 23rd, 2012). Ibrahima Thioub asserts the following:

> Entre les XVe et XVIIIe siècles, les Européens n'avaient pas les moyens politiques et militaires d'aller chercher les esclaves eux-mêmes. (...) Ils n'avaient pas les moyens de soigner des maladies particulièrement meurtrières, comme la maladie du sommeil ou la malaria. Une armée européenne qui se serait aventurée dans les terres en Afrique aurait été très rapidement décimée. Les Européens doivent donc rester sur la côte et attendre que des commerçants africains leur amènent les marchandises dont ils ont besoin. Ces commerçants autochtones servaient d'intermédiaires avec les compagnies européennes. Ils étaient de connivence avec les Etats africains, eux-mêmes souvent très militarisés.
>
> Between the fifteen and eighteenth centuries, Europeans did not have the political and military means to get the slaves themselves. (...) They do not have the means to treat highly lethal diseases, such as sleeping sickness and malaria. A European army which would have ventured into the interior of Africa would have been quickly decimated. Europeans must stay on the coast and wait for African traders to deliver the goods they need. These indigenous merchants acted as intermediaries with European companies. They colluded with the African states which were often heavily militarized. (My translation).

Ibrahima Thioub's claim that the Africans bear a heavy responsibility in the transatlantic slave trade is echoed by Alain Mabanckou in his book, *Le sanglot de l'Homme noir*. The Congolese writer explains in his book, in particular in the chapter "Le devoir de violence", that black slaves were often captured and sold into slavery by either other blacks or Arabs. In this regard, in his contribution to the *magazine Slate Afrique* in March 16th, 2012, Mabanckou takes a firm position about the answerability of Africans in the slave trade. He states:

> Pourtant, il serait inexact d'affirmer que le blanc capturait tout seul le noir pour le réduire en esclavage. La part de responsabilité des Noirs dans la traite négrière reste un tabou parmi les Africains, qui refusent d'ordinaire de se regarder dans un miroir.

> Yet it would be inaccurate to say that the White captured alone for the Black enslavement. The responsibility of blacks in the slave trade remains a taboo among the Africans, who usually refuse to look at themselves in a mirror. (My translation).

Historians like Ibrahima Thioub and Alain Mabanckou invite us to look critically at history so as to get to the core of the historical reality. Ellison when asking the question about which historian is going to record Tod Clifton's crime is calling for historians like Alain Mabanckou and Ibrahima Thioub whose prime concern is to get the historical reality out whether it incriminates his own race or not. That is what "devoir de mémoire" is all about.

Then to engage with Nadel's reading of Clifton's chapter as a passage about betrayal, including the betrayer and the betrayed, we can argue that the loyalties to "devoir de mémoire" require that the answerability of Africans be told otherwise the meaning of betrayal would depend upon them, the African historians and writers who are mouthpieces of their communities. As I have mentioned earlier, the only history that may be viewed as shameful or tragic is the one muted because it will circle back. Yet, I think like Mabanckou that the past should not be rehashed to the point that it prevents the Africans from moving forward.

On balance, if we take into consideration the fact that the same ideology of "blackwash" that permeates Ellison's text (the refusal of home to raise and discuss its answerability in the history of slavery) exists in Morrison's text, Patricia's refusal to include Africa in her curriculum means that whatever curriculum we may put in place, something essential will be left out. In other words, the curriculum will be either a victim of whitewash or a victim of blackwash or, worse, both. Reverent Richard Misner's stand to history is similar to Mabanckou's. Reverent Richard Misner takes an emotional distance from the past, in so doing he succeeds in learning from it and in forgiving, which is not the case with Patricia. Patricia has lost "the reconciling power of forgiveness". Indeed, as Derrida teaches us "... all is forgivable except the crime against spirit, that is, against the reconciling power of forgiveness" (34). When you forgive you reach out to your perpetrator or betrayer. You don't shut him or her off. Patricia's stand metaphorizes well the Antilles' repression of ancestry.

Healing the wound of "the unmentionable past":

Does postmemory extend to the heirs of the perpetrator? Mariann Hirsh does not discuss this point. Woodard, when analyzing Clinton, Bush, and Obama's visits to the slave fort in Senegal, reminds us that they did not apologize despite their moving addresses. Woodard presents the visits of the three presidents in this passage:

> In unprecedented visits at Senegal's House of Slaves, then sitting-US presidents Bill Clinton, George Bush, and Barack Obama in 1998, 2003, and 2013, respectively, ceded the international heritage site as a magnet for discussion about apologies, reparations, and responsibility for the Atlantic slave trade, yet none of them discussed the role of the US in that trade. (The presidents had followed luminaries to the site at Gorée that include Pope John Paul II and Nelson Mandela, former South African.) Clinton, as the first US president to make the journey, proclaimed profound regret in a well-publicized address over the horrors of the Atlantic slave trade. But reportedly fearing liability for slave reparations, he did not issue an apology for the nation's role in that trade. (p. 21)

In the case of president Obama, as a diasporic subject, the scenario changes. Is he in the same position like President Clinton and Bush to ask for forgiveness on behalf of the US for the role it played in that trade? Instead, the continental Africans have to ask for forgiveness to him regardless of whether or not he is entitled to ask for forgiveness on behalf of the US government. But the continental Africans did not do that either. Ironically, they welcome him as the returning brother, in so doing renewing "the myth of return" as Woodard suggests. Both Clinton and Bush have to measure the consequences of asking for forgiveness against the staled statu quo of guilty silence. Herein, the rhetoric of silence that characterizes slavery, as Hubert Gerbeau articulates, sets in. Before the diasporic subject Obama, the regional Africans face a conundrum about how to ask for forgiveness. Indeed, as Gates points out, in his op-ed "The Future of Slavery's Past," the answerability of Africans would make the issue of reparation, which is a potential outcome of an apology, problematic. Therefore, the regional Africans, much like Bush and Clinton, are more inclined to ignore the issue of forgiveness and hail Obama as the returning brother. When we read these three apology scenarios in the light of Hirsch's postmemory theory, it seems that postmemory does not extend to the heirs of the victimizer or perpetrator. But Morrison with the Tuskegee syphilis study shows that the heirs of a crime have to apologize. Since in the real story where she gets her inspiration from for *Home*, President Clinton apologizes. He intones: "What was done cannot be undone. But we can end the silence. We can stop turning our heads away. We can look at you in the eye and finally say on behalf of the American people, what the United States government did was shameful, and I am sorry."

As we recall, *Home* draws on the Tuskegee Syphilis Study. The Tuskegee Syphilis Study is a study in which American physicians deliberately injected Syphilis and other diseases into African Americans to see how these diseases would evolve over time in humans. Morrison fictionalizes this dehumanizing historical event through the various experimentations on the bodies of African Americans. The disease which is injected into the body of African Americans can also be read figuratively, Laura Castor through a pun, writes "dis-ease" to highlight the state of uncomfort and hostility of minority groups in America. In terms of narrative structure, there are multi-layered truths, point of views, and narrations in *Home*, which creates a conflation or superimposition of histories. But Morrison in her text leaves out the lawsuit against the doctors, President Bill Clinton's apology, and the reparation. Yet one thing that she tries to faithfully render is the long period of silence before the crime breaks out, forty years passed by before the syphilis study become known. The unreliability of the narration and the self-doubtful narrators are meant to create breaks in the linear narrative to capture the silences in the history of the Tuskegee Syphilis Study. Also, by leaving out the lawsuit against the doctors, President Bill Clinton's apology, and the reparation in her fiction of the Tuskegee Syphilis Study, Morrison demonstrates that if her fiction captures completely and accurately a historical event, her text becomes closer to a history book than to a piece of fiction. A piece of fiction leaves out gaps for the reader to fill in. And, it is obvious that by leaving out the issues of the lawsuit against the doctors, President Bill Clinton's apology, and the reparation, Morrison mimics, too, the way through which the historiography has erased African American history from collective memory and the archives.

Contrary to President Bush and Clinton, John Paul II in his 1992 visit to Senegal's house of slave asked for forgiveness. He asks: "How can one forget the enormous suffering inflicted, ignoring the most elementary rights of man, on the people deported from the African continent?" before concluding with "From this African sanctuary of black pain, we begged the pardon from above." John Paul II asks for forgiveness on behalf of the Christians involved in the slave trade. Besides, as an embodiment of a religious institution, John Paul II is in a more propitious position to do so. Albeit the issues of reparations are less at stake through John Paul II's apology, he has given an opportunity for healing and reconciliation. Much the same is true with Clinton's apology for the Tuskegee Syphilis Study. Morrison let Clinton's apology function as a paratext within her fictionalized Tuskegee Syphilis Study, therefore she does not avail herself the opportunity to discuss it in the novel. But Clinton's address is worth analyzing since it is steeped in *Sankofa*. When Clinton apologizes there were only six survivors remaining out of the 201 subjects that's why he insists on learning from the past. He says:

> The United States government did something that was wrong – deeply, profoundly, morally wrong… It is not only in remembering that shameful past that we can make amends and repair our nation, but it is in remembering that past that we can build a better present and a better future.

Clinton's apology interrupts "the ordinary course of historical temporality" (p. 32), which is one of the attributes of forgiveness as Derrida articulates. Besides, Clinton's address sets the tone for the heir of a victimizer who wants to acknowledge and repair the wrongs of the past. If he were to apologize during his visit to the slave house at Gorée his address would have been formulated the same way. Similarly, if the Africans were to apologize before President Obama during his visit, their address would have been modelled after that of Clinton. That is to say acknowledging their answerability and formally asking for forgiveness, and proposing a symbolic means of reparation like the Sankofa transatlantic slavery monument that I am advocating here.

Also, when analyzing the enigma of apology, Derrida explains that a third person should not intervene since as soon as a third person intervenes, we can no longer talk about forgiveness but rather amnesty. In other words, like the apology that John Paul II formulated, it was genuine and spontaneous, no one asked him let alone compelled him to do so. His desire for forgiveness came from within. So, in the case of Obama, the same impulse should have driven the Africans to ask for forgiveness. In the same vein, the same impulse should have prompted Clinton and Bush to do the same. But in his analysis of the enigma of forgiveness, Derrida alludes to an issue without truly elaborating on it. Does forgiveness really heal the wound? Derrida writes: "In the radical evil of which we are speaking, and consequently in the enigma of the forgiveness of the unforgivable, there is a sort of 'madness' which the juridico-political cannot approach, much less appropriate." (P. 55) The ability to forgive or not to forgive remains a matter of the heart and therefore, it is out of the reach of the sphere of the juridico-political. In other words, to forgive or not to forgive is a personal decision that should not be mediated. That's why Derrida says as soon as there is mediation, we can no longer speak of "pure forgiveness in the strict sense." (p. 42) The person wronged can't ask his or her perpetrator to ask for forgiveness. In the same vein, it behooves to the person wronged to decide whether or not to forgive. But for the case of monstrous crimes like genocides or slavery, the heads of State of the parties involved can legitimately call upon forgiveness on behalf of their nations. Despite all these paradigms of forgiveness, forgiveness can break "the ordinary course of historical temporality" (p. 32), which is the real stepping stone to forgiveness. Breaking the silence around slavery across the Atlantic is in itself healing.

Indeed, when speaking about American slavery, the historian Lonnie Bunch asserts that "American slavery is one of the last great unmentionables in public discourse" (p. 11) (as quoted by Markus Nehl). This statement applies as much to American slavery as it applies to African slavery. To perpetuate this erasure of slavery from public discourse and collective African memory, the African discourse of slavery has been and still is two dimensional, involving only the responsibility of Europeans and Americans putting that of Africans out of the picture. It is this narrative that refuses to apportion the blame a bit on oneself and a bit on the Other that Achille Mbembe calls "African Modes of Self Writing". Such a representation makes the transnational dimension of the history of slavery skewed in the sense that it thickens "the shadowy zone that conceals deep silence" to echo Achille Mbembe. But as Hartman informs us there has to be an "ethics of historical representation of slavery." To create a space where healing and reconciliation can take place between regional Africans and Africans of the diaspora, such as a mode of self-writing has to be superseded by a narrative that engages with neo-slave narratives and current memory and diaspora studies across the globe.

Forgiveness or reconciliation always presents itself as a dilemma; it takes the form of a double imperative. Forgiveness has to be genuine and unconditional as Derrida argues. Also, as Simon Critchley and Richard Kearney paraphrase it in their preface to Derrida's book: "if forgiveness forgave only the forgivable, then, Derrida claims, the very idea of forgiveness would disappear. It has to consist in the attempt to forgive the unforgivable: whether the murderousness of Apartheid or the Shoah." (p. VII) Derrida's argument is hard to reject since for a world scale crime like slavery forgiveness has to be unconditional. Yet there is a condition upon which this unconditional forgiveness hinges: the reconstitution of the historical truth. In fact, as I have argued the only history can be viewed as shameful is the one silenced since it runs the risk of repeating itself.

Conclusion

The truth is what hurts but let's answer to its call

Slavery is such an emotive and controversial issue that reconstituting the historical truth becomes a Sisyphus task. The authenticity of slave sites such as Gorée in Senegal and Elmina castle in Ghana are well discussed by Woodard in *Slave Sites on Display*. Slave sites are historical artefacts that are supposed to reveal the highest truth about what happened. And yet, they suffer from the "archive fever." In this respect, Woodard writes, "Silences and omissions in certain "official" records have failed to account for the particularities of what happened to the enslaved Africans, their ancestors, and their progeny, and have therefore opened up a space for legends to take root." (p. 32) These silences and omissions in the archival records have allowed room for a manipulation of the historical truth. In the light of this existing shadowy zone, can we talk about healing and reconciliation? Indeed, as Woodard explains, for scholars interested in the history of slavery, particularly Africans of the diaspora, there is a burning desire to know and the unbearable pain of being unable to know exactly the historical truth. This situation leads to a double conundrum. In order to forgive, the slave descendants on both sides of the Atlantic have to know the historical truth, so they can learn from it and forgive and call upon forgiveness. In other words, is the slave descendant who is suffering from the impossibility of not knowing in a position to sit on the table of reconciliation and forgiveness. Derrida, in his work, contends that forgiveness has to be granted even to the one who does not ask for it. Yet, in the context of slavery can we grant forgiveness to the one who conceals the evidence that would allow such an opportunity to take place. Within this dilemma, reconciliation and forgiveness can only happen through a postmodern Black Atlantic truth and reconciliation commission built on the image of the South African Truth and Reconciliation Commission. UNESCO which has funded the restoration of many slave forts can initiate the postmodern Black Atlantic truth and reconciliation commission which will lead to the building of a Sankofa transatlantic slavery monument. UNESCO will simply act as a symbolic institution since as Derrida informs us "…one only forgives where one can judge and punish, therefore, evaluate, then the putting into place, the institution of an instance of judgement, supposes a power, a force, a sovereignty." (p. 59) Through the creation of a postmodern Black Atlantic truth and reconciliation commission, the curtains of blackwash and whitewash that block or obscure the open academic and public discourse about slavery in the continent and outside of it will be torn down. In so doing, we will answer to Wright's rallying cry when he utters at the beginning of the twentieth century:

> One of the greatest ironies of the twentieth century is that when communication has reached its zenith, when the human voice can encircle the globe in a matter of seconds, when man can project the image of his face thousands of miles, it is almost impossible to know with any degree of accuracy the truth of a political situation only a hundred miles distant! Propaganda jams the media of communication. (p. 100)

In the same vein, after answering to Wright's rallying cry, we will have to answer to Caryl Phillip's call in *Crossing the River* when he invites us to take care of the diaspora slave descendants. Maria Rice Bellamy sums up Phillip's call this passage:

> Phillips uses the African father's words and the white characters' responses to the abandoned children to model how those who initiated and benefited from the transatlantic slave trade can take responsibility for the children of the African diaspora, restore their humanity and finally earn the privilege of celebrating their survival, as seen in the epilogue. (p. 131)

Such a statement is ripe for reflection for Africana and African diaspora studies scholars and policy makers regardless of which side of the Atlantic you reside.

Also, as already pointed out, Woodard compares slave sites to both womb and tomb. To stretch this metaphor with a view to connecting it to the enigma of the forgiveness of the unforgivable, it can be argued that like the physical womb which can expand to take a lot despite its tiny nature in the midst of the woman, it always allows room for forgiveness. It bleeds at times and renews itself. The slave site as a womb has to enable such a renewal between continental Africans and diaspora slave descendants. Therefore, let's answer to Derrida's call that pure forgiveness is unconditional and granted even to the one who does not ask for it.

Sources cited

Temple, Christel N. "The Emergence of Sankofa Practice in the United States: A Modern History." Journal of Black Studies, Vol. 41, No. 1 (September 2010), pp. 127-150 (24 pages).

Richard Wright, *The Color Curtain*. Jackson: University Press of Mississippi. 1994.

Victor, L. Simpson. "Pope Visits Slave Isle, Asks Forgiveness". AP News, February, 22, 1992.

Bellamy, Maria Rice. "Haunting the African Diaspora: Responsibility and Remaining in Caryl Phillips's "Crossing the River."" *African American Review*, Spring 2014, Vol. 47, No. 1 (Spring 2014), pp. 129-144.

Bhabha, Homi. "The World and the Home". Third World and Post-colonial Issues, Number 31- 32. 1992.

Hirsch, Marianne. "The Generation of Postmemory". *Poetics Today,* 29:1 (Spring, pp.103-128). 2008.

Newton, Adam Zachary. *Facing Black and Jew: Literature as Public Space in Twentieth-Century America.* Cambridge University Press, UK. 1999.

Jamali, Leyli and Razmi Mehri. " Magic(al) Realism as Postcolonial Device in Toni Morrison's *Beloved."* International Journal of Humanities and Social Science Vol. 2 No. 5; March 2012.

Gates, Henry Louis Jr. ''The Future of Slavery's Past.'' New York Times, 29 juillet, 2001.

Sandra Crouse Quinn, "Presidential Apology for the Study at Tuskegee", Britannica: May 16, 1997.

Nehl, Markus. *Transnational Black Dialogues: Re-imagining Slavery in the Twenty-First Century. Postcolonial Studies*, Volume 28, 2016 (p. 212).

Murphy, Laura T. *Metaphor and the Slave Trade in West African Literature.* Athens: Ohio University Press, 2012.

Derrida, Jacques. *Archive Fever: A Freudian Impression*. Trans. Eric Prenowitz. Chicago: U of Chicago P, 1996.

Huyssen, Andreas. *Twilight Memories: Marking Time in a Culture of Amnesia.* London: Routlegde, 1995.

Crownshaw, Richard. *Reconsidering Postmemory: Photography, the Archive, and Post-Holocaust Memory in W.G. Sebald's ''Austerlitz''. Mosaic:*

An Interdisciplinary Critical Journal, vol.37, No. 4, special issue: THE PHOTOGRAPH. December, 2004, pp.215-236.

Hirsch, Marianne. *"Surviving Images: Holocaust Photograph and the Work of Postmemory." Yale Journal of Criticism* 12.1 Spring (2001): pp.5-37.

Ba, Cheikh Oumar et Ndiaye Alfred Iniss. "L'émigration clandestine sénégalaise," REVUE Asylon(s), No. 3, Mars 2008, Migrations et Sénégal., url de référence: http://www.reseau-terra.eu/article717.html

Sarai, Esha. "Ethnic Conflicts in Mali Exacerbated by Extremist Presence,"Voanews.com, June 14, 2019. (https://www.voanews.com/africa/ethnic-conflicts- mali-exacerbated-extremist-presence).

Lonnie Bunch, "The Director of the African-American History and Culture Museum on What Makes '12 Years a Slave' a Powerful Film," *The Smithsonian.com* 5 Nov. 2013, 26 July 2015 http://www.smithsonianmag.com/ist/?next=/smithsonian-institution/the-director-of-the-african-american-history-and-culture-museum-on-what-makes- 12-years-a-slave-a-powerful-film-180947568/.

Saidiya Hartman, "Venus in Two Acts," *Small Axe* 12.2 (2008): 5.

Hubert Gerbeau, *Les Esclaves noirs: Pour une histoire du silence*. Editeur, Indes savants, Collection Rivages de Xantons, Paris, 2013.

Daniel, Maragnes. «L'identité et le désastre. Origine et fondation», Portulan no. 98 (n. d.), a special issue devoted to «Mémoire juive, mémoire nègre. Deux figures du destin». Publié le 4 janvier 2008.

Bhabha, Homi. "The World and the Home". Third World and Post-colonial Issues, Number 31- 32. 1992.

Castor, Laura in *Toni Morrison: Critical Theoretical Approaches*. Nancy J. Peterson, editor. Baltimore: The John Hopkins U.P., 1997.

Bauer, Camille. Interview with Ibrahima Thioub in *Parti de Gauche Midi*. 23 Janvier 2012.

Alain, Mabanckou. *Le Sanglot de l'Homme Noir*. Paris: Editions Fayard. 2012.

Aimé, Césaire. *Discourse on Colonialism*, translated by Joan Pinkham. Monthly Review Press: New York. 2000.

Derrida, Jacques. *On Cosmopolitanism and Forgiveness,* translated by Mark Dooley and Michael Hughes. Routledge: London and New York. 2005.

Eichstedt, L. Jennifer and Small Stephen. *Representations of Slavery: Race and Ideology in Southern Plantation Museums*. New York: Smithsonian Institution Press. September 2002.

Ellison, Ralph. *Shadow and Act*. New York. Vintage Books, 1972.

----------, Ralph. *Invisible Man*. New York: Vintage International.1990.

---------, Ralph. *Juneteenth* (edited by J.F. Callahan). Hamish Hamilton: London. 1999.

Gates, Henry Louis, Jr. *The Signifying Monkey: A Theory of African-American Literary Criticism*. Oxford: Oxford U.P.1988.

Gilroy, Paul. *The Black Atlantic*. Oxford: Oxford U.P. 1993.

Greene, J. L. *Blacks in Eden*. Virginia: U.P. of Virginia.1996.

Hirsch, Marianne. "The Generation of Postmemory". *Poetics Today,* 29:1 (Spring, pp.103-128). 2008.

Hobson, Z. Christopher. "Ralph Ellison's Juneteenth and African American Identity," *The Utopian*, Vol. 2, 2001.

Hutton, Patrick. "Recent Scholarship on Memory and History." *The History Teacher*. Volume 33, Number 4, August 2000.

Jameson, Fredric. *The Political Unconscious: Narrative as a Socially Symbolic Act*. Ithaca, New York: Cornell U.P.1982.

Jones, Jacqueline. "Fact and Fiction in Alice Walker's *The Color Purple*." *The Georgia Historical Quarterly* Vol. LXXII, No. 4, Winter 1988.

Mabanckou, Alain. « Les Africains ont une responsabilité dans la traite des Noirs. » Le Magazine *Slate Afrique*. 16 Mars 2012.

Morrison, Toni. " Rootedness: The Ancestor as Foundation" in Mari Evans. Ed, *The Black Women Writers: A Critical Evaluation*. Doubleday: New York. 1984.

------------, Toni. *Playing in the Dark*. New York: Vintage Books.1997.

------------, Toni. *Song of Solomon*. New York: Signet. 1977.

------------, Toni. *Playing in the Dark: Whiteness and the Literary Imagination*. New York: Vintage, 1992.

------------, Toni. "Rootedness: The Ancestors as Foundation." *In Black Women Writers*1950-1980, edited by Mari Evans, 339-45. London: Pluto, 1985.

------------, Toni. *Paradise*. Alfred A. Knopf, New York - Toronto, 1998.

------------, Toni. *Beloved*. Vintage International: Vintage Books, Random House, Inc. New York, 2004.

Newton, Adam Zachary. *Facing Black and Jew: Literature as Public Space in Twentieth-Century America*. Cambridge University Press, UK. 1999.

Nora, Pierre. "Between Memory and History: Les Lieux de Mémoires." *Representations*. Number 26, Special Issue: Memory and Counter-Memory (pp. 7- 24), Spring,1989.

O'Meally, Robert Ed. *New Essays on Invisible Man*. Cambridge: Cambridge U.P. 1988.

-------------, Robert G. *The Craft of Ralph Ellison*. Cambridge Massachusetts: Harvard U.P.1980.

Peterson, J. Nancy. *Against Amnesia: Contemporary Women Writers and the Crises of Historical Memory*. Philadelphia: U.P of Pennsylvania Press. 2002.

Walker, Alice. *The Color Purple*. New York. 1982.

Zelizer, Barbie. "Reading the Past Against the Grain: The Shape of Memory Studies." *Critical Studies in Mass Communication*. Volume 12, Issue 2, 1995.

Bakhtin, M. Mikhailovich. *The Dialogic Imagination: Four Essays by Bakhtin*. Michael Holquist ed. (translated by Caryl Emerson & Michael Holquist). Austin: University of Texas Press. 1981.

Richards, Sandra L. "Notes from the Road: Cultural Tourism to Slave Sites," BTNews, Vol 9. No 2&3, Winter/Spring1999.

Nix, Elizabeth. "Tuskegee Experiment: The Infamous Syphilis Study," history.com, May 16, 2017. (https://www.history.com/news/the-infamous-40-year-tuskegee-study)

Dye, T. R. *Understanding Public Policy*. New Jersey, NJ: Pearson Prentice Hall. 2012.

Mamdani, Mahmood. *Citizen and Subject: Contemporary Africa and the Legacy of Late Colonialism*. Princeton: Princeton University Press. 2018.

ANSD Data: (https://www.ansd.sn/ressources/ses/chapitres/1-SES-2016_Etat-structure-population.pdf, 2 Mai 2021.

Smith, Étienne and Labrune, Céline. *Les hussards noirs de la colonie - instituteurs africains et petites patries en AOF, 1913-1960*. Paris: KARTHALA, 16 May 2018.

www.ingramcontent.com/pod-product-compliance
Lightning Source LLC
Chambersburg PA
CBHW071941240426
43669CB00048B/2545